Housing
First

Housing First

The Pathways Model to End Homelessness for People with Mental Illness and Addiction

Sam Tsemberis, Ph.D.

HAZELDEN®

Hazelden
Center City, Minnesota 55012
hazelden.org

Library of Congress Cataloging-in-Publication Data

Tsemberis, Sam J.
  Housing first : the Pathways model to end homelessness for people with mental illness and addiction / Sam Tsemberis.
     p. cm.
  Includes bibliographical references and index.
  ISBN 978-1-59285-998-6
  1. Homeless persons--Housing--United States. 2. Homeless persons--Housing. 3. Homeless persons--Services for--United States. 4. Mentally ill homeless persons--Services for--United States. 5. Homeless persons--Substance use--United States. I. Title.
  HV4505.T74 2010
  363.5'9740973--dc22

                    2010035376

Editor's note: The names, details, and circumstances may have been changed to protect the privacy of those mentioned in this publication.

The suggestions and model documents in this book are not meant to substitute for the advice of lawyers, accountants, or other professionals.

Cover design by David Spohn
Interior design and typesetting by David Farr, ImageSmythe

to Cherie, Elena, and Alex
who taught me about love

and for every person who came to Pathways to Housing
from the streets, hospitals, and jails—
and never lost the ability to love

Contents

Chapter 2

Initial Program Steps   33

Chapter 3

Housing and Housing Support Services   47

Foreword

SOME PEOPLE, CONVINCED ON PRINCIPLE, "get" the idea of Housing First instantly. Others are more skeptical, convinced by their training that people with mental illnesses and substance abuse problems are incapable of making wise decisions for themselves. In 1998, I was part of the team conducting the first experimental evaluation of Pathways Housing First. Founder Sam Tsemberis—everyone calls him Sam—had already shown in two published studies that Pathways tenants were more stable in their housing than clients in other programs designed for people with long histories of homelessness and serious psychiatric disabilities. Traditionally trained social service providers from the other programs, which required clients to be clean and sober and participate in treatment in order to have a bed of their own in a congregate facility, claimed that Sam must be working with a different group of people—that their clients could not succeed in a model where homeless people are given independent apartments with a panoply of services but without close supervision. It seemed time to put Sam's model to a more rigorous test, randomly assigning some people to Pathways to Housing and others to traditional programs to create a fair comparison.

Recruitment to the study was lagging, so we held a breakfast for outreach workers to explain the experiment and to urge them to refer more people. One outreach worker ate our bagels but argued that it would not be ethical to refer the clients she worked with to the study: they might get randomly assigned to *receive their own apartment*, and that, she insisted, would be setting them up for failure. A couple weeks later, we caught a break. A study participant who had been randomly assigned to Pathways to Housing invited his family and his former outreach worker over to dinner to show off his new apartment. The outreach worker was so impressed by the transformation of the disheveled denizen of the street into a gracious host that he told all the other workers at his agency. They responded by referring dozens of clients to the study, and we finished up recruitment with a bang.

Of course, the outreach worker's epiphany could have been based on an anomalous case. But the evidence from the study was convincing: over the first year, people randomly assigned to the Pathways program spent ninety-nine fewer days homeless than individuals in the control group, and used substances at no greater rates. Pathways participants got housed faster and stayed housed longer. The enormous differences between experimental and control groups gradually narrowed over time as more control group members found their way indoors, but a study published in 2004 found that the Pathways tenants were still far more likely to be housed at the end of the four-year experiment. Nonetheless, I have no way of knowing whether the skeptical outreach worker at that breakfast was convinced.

By now, Housing First has garnered so much acclaim that everyone claims to be doing it, no matter how little their programs resemble the Pathways to Housing model. Pathways Housing First is neither a "housing only" approach, nor does it offer "worker-knows-best" services coupled with immediate housing. It is a successful, rigorously documented, systematic approach to serving homeless people with addiction and mental health disorders. This manual clarifies the ethos and practices of Pathways Housing First. Hopefully, it will also begin to change the standard training that still makes it hard for many social service professionals to give up coercive control—no matter how artfully it may be disguised—and support the choices of the people with whom they work.

Marybeth Shinn, Ph.D.
Professor and Chair
Department of Human and Organizational Development
Vanderbilt University

Acknowledgments

THIS BOOK OWES ITS EXISTENCE to the many remarkable people, past and present, whom I met as clients served by Pathways to Housing and its predecessors, Choices Unlimited and the 44th Street Independence Support Center drop-in centers. By bringing together the essential elements of our many heated and passionate conversations about choice, power, rights, poverty, privacy, disabilities, and abilities, we were able to develop, design, implement, and operate the Pathways Housing First program. I had the good fortune to have Bill Anthony, David Shern, Mikal Cohen, and Howie the Harp as early collaborators in our "taking psych rehab to the streets" grant. Our 44th Street drop-in center was modeled after Howie's consumer-operated Independence Support Center in Oakland. Rachel Efron, Hilary Melton, and Ed Rooney were influential staff members who ensured that our priority lay in taking care of the needs of our clients, and not of the programs.

In the early nineties, when Housing First was considered a risky venture, Bert Pepper, Mary Brosnahan, and Elmer Struening, national experts in mental health and advocates for ending homelessness, risked their reputations in order to support our work by joining our board. Since then, Housing First has been replicated in hundreds of cities by innumerable local champions who have started Pathways programs in their own communities. In recent years, we've had welcome support from Philip Mangano, Ann O'Hara, and Nan Roman, all of whom have been prolific advocates for using Housing First as a means of abolishing what Mangano has called "the national disgrace of homelessness."

There were many lessons learned from early program replications, the ones that took place when most providers could still not believe that with the right support people with psychiatric disabilities could live on their own in their own apartments. These replications—the ones created before the evidence base was available—were the most challenging and required the greatest investment from our stakeholders. It took enormous courage for Nancy Travers to import the program into Westchester County. Marti Kinsley had the political will and willingness to risk importing Pathways to Washington, DC. The program in the nation's capital would not have been possible without Nan Roman's advocacy and the generosity of the Abell Foundation. In the early years, my friend and writing mentor Jay Neugeboren put our program on the national map by describing it in his book *Transforming Madness: New Lives for People Living with Mental Illness.*

This book would not have been possible without the ingenious researchers who conducted the rigorous longitudinal randomized controlled trials that have charted the development and effectiveness of Pathways as an evidence-based program. This group includes Sara Asmussen, Beth Shinn, and especially Ana Stefancic, our director of research, who also provided the research summary for this volume. Their articles led to program dissemination that created hundreds of Housing First programs that have, across the country, succeeded in ending homelessness for many thousands of people.

Today, the Mental Health Commission of Canada is at the midpoint of a $110 million, longitudinal randomized controlled trial to test the effectiveness of our Housing First program in five Canadian cities. This is an unprecedented and enormous social science experiment, and it is a great honor to be working with a talented Canadian team that includes Paula Goering, who directs the research, and Jayne Barker and Cam Keller, who direct the project at the Commission. I am grateful to Tim Richter, director of the Calgary Homeless Foundation and advocate for the Housing First approach. With Tim's able assistance and the collaboration of our colleagues at the Alex Community Health Centre, we were awarded a knowledge dissemination grant from the Canadian government. I am extremely indebted to all my Canadian compatriots because my participation in their projects, and what I learned as a participant, have helped make the writing of this book possible.

The Canadian programs have fewer fiscal constraints then those in the United States. In part because Canadians have national health insurance, the financial operations of our programs in Canada have few restrictions placed upon them. This creates an environment where funding does not impinge upon clinical practice (e.g., requiring a fixed number of visits per client in order to be reimbursed). It became easy to see, and thus to be able to describe, how it is possible for the Pathways Housing First program to operate across a wide variety of settings. Juliana Walker, our director of training, who works with me on the Canadian projects, contributed enormously to this volume by writing early drafts, editing others, and helping to clarify and describe various aspects of team operations.

Bob Drake, my friend and colleague at Dartmouth, has been supportive of our program. Among other things, Bob helped Ana Stefancic and me as we shaped the research on program fidelity. But a book needs a publisher, and Bob introduced me to Sid Farrar of Hazelden Publishing. Sid's enthusiasm, and his professionalism, made the process painless and efficient. I am most grateful to Cynthia Orange, my editor at Hazelden who suggested changes in structure and content that have improved the book and made it readable, and who offered invaluable guidance, along with a gentle therapeutic touch, throughout our collaboration. Thank you, too, to Mindy Keskinen—you brought it all together and took it to the finish line.

Above all, I want to acknowledge the support and love I receive from my wife, Cherie, and our children Elena and Alex. Their patience during family vacations and other times that I have had to spend away from them, and their acceptance and understanding, have made it possible for me to complete this project. Most summers we visit *yiayia* (my mother; my children's grandmother) in Skoura, a village in southern Greece. In this village of some five hundred people, everyone is included in *kafenio* at the center of town: old and young, rich and poor, some with mental health problems and some without. It is a place where there is respect and acceptance of all—just as it is at Pathways to Housing.

All royalties from the sale of this book will be contributed to Pathways to Housing.

Introduction

As originators of the Housing First model, Pathways to Housing seeks to transform individual lives by ending homelessness and supporting recovery for those with psychiatric disabilities and co-occurring addiction disorders. We believe housing is a basic human right and aspire to change the practice of homeless services by

- *providing immediate access to permanent independent apartments, without preconditions for psychiatric treatment or sobriety*

- *setting the standard for services driven by consumer choice that support recovery and community integration*

- *conducting research to find innovative solutions and best practices for those who suffer from mental illness and addiction*

Pathways to Housing, Inc. mission statement (adapted)

Homelessness: A Global Problem

People with psychiatric disabilities who are also homeless can be found worldwide. Their characteristics vary from country to country, and so do the reasons for their homelessness. But the problems they face because of their shared conditions give them more in common than the differences that divide them. Access to affordable housing and treatment is an almost universal barrier for this population worldwide. Estimating the number of people who are homeless and who have mental illness presents complex methodological and epidemiological challenges because definitions of homelessness and mental illness vary across countries and across cultures. The United Nations provides a practical and useful definition:

> The correct definition of a homeless household should be. . . "those households [or individuals] without a shelter that would fall within the scope of living quarters. They carry their few possessions with them, sleeping in streets, in doorways, or on piers, or in any other space, on a more or less random basis."[1]

Further complications arise because counting the number of people who are homeless and have psychiatric disabilities is not simply a matter of identifying individual or demographic characteristics of this population. This number can also be viewed as an index of a nation's failed social service, housing, and mental health policies. Thus, the number of people who are homeless can be seen as a consequence of larger social problems. Research on the *Gini coefficient* is one way to illustrate this point. This coefficient is a commonly used measure of a nation's income disparity—the distance between rich and poor. A 2000 World Health Organization study reported that developed European countries and Canada had Gini indices between .24 and .36, while the United States and Mexico were both at .46 and Brazil and South Africa at .61. Of relevance here is that social scientists report that there is a negative correlation between the Gini coefficient and the percentage of a nation's budget spent on social and mental health services.[2] Countries whose social and mental health policies provide financial and other support to those at the bottom of the income distribution are also the countries with lower levels of homelessness.[3] It is not surprising that, in general, advocates accuse governments of underestimating the number of homeless, and government representatives say that advocates tend to overestimate. For example, the United States Department of Housing and Urban Development (HUD) conducts a nationwide "one-night count" of the homeless every year. The count is conducted late at night in the middle of winter. In 2007, the most recent year for which data is available, HUD estimated 670,000 people were homeless—staying on the streets or in drop-in centers, shelters, or temporary housing.[4] This number is equivalent to the population of cities like Boston, Memphis, or Baltimore. In that same year, the advocacy organization National Law Center on Homelessness and Poverty estimated the number of homeless at 3.5 million.[5] In another national survey of the prevalence of homelessness, Bruce Link and his colleagues estimated that 26 million persons had been homeless at one point in their lives.[6] As for the subpopulation that is the focus of this manual, HUD estimated in 2008 that 28 percent of the people who are homeless have severe mental illness; 39 percent have chronic substance abuse issues; and 18 percent are considered "chronically homeless," which means they have been continuously homeless for over one year and suffer from mental or physical disabilities.[7] Those figures are consistent with other studies that estimate a 30 to 70 percent incidence of mental health problems among the homeless, with the highest percentages among the chronically homeless.

A 2007 study of mental health and homelessness by the Canadian Institute for Health Information estimated that more than 10,000 people are homeless on any given night across Canada.[8] The report also found that mental disorders accounted for 52 percent of acute care hospitalizations among Canadian homeless in 2005 and 2006. Because of the data collection complexities in its many member countries, measuring homelessness in the European Union (EU) is even more difficult than in the United States. However, the European Federation of National Organizations Working with the Homeless (FEANTSA) estimated that at least 3 million Western Europeans were homeless during the winter of 2003.[9]

From our perspective as clinicians and advocates, any number of people who have severe psychiatric disabilities and are living on the streets is too big a number. Once people enter into homelessness, they are at greatly increased risk for health problems, victimization, malnutrition, exhaustion, and exacerbation of psychiatric and addiction disorders. Their physical and mental health deteriorates rapidly, and those who remain chronically homeless are among the most vulnerable. Fortunately, as Pathways to Housing has discovered and this manual will show, the problems encountered by people who have remained homeless and who have multiple or co-occurring conditions are problems with a proven solution—a solution called "Housing First."

About Housing First and This Manual

Housing First ends homelessness. It's that simple.

—Sam Tsemberis, founder and CEO
of Pathways to Housing, Inc.

Founded in 1992 in New York City, Pathways to Housing, Inc. is a nonprofit corporation that is widely credited as being the originator of the Housing First model
of addressing homelessness among people with mental health and addiction
problems. Put simply, Pathways' unique approach is this: provide housing first,
and then combine that housing with supportive services and treatment services.
Research studies examining this model have shown that it dramatically reduces
homelessness and is significantly more effective than traditional treatment and
housing models. Because the Pathways model is so distinctive—providing services
through a consumer-driven treatment philosophy and providing scattered-site
housing in independent apartments—we refer to it as the Pathways Housing
First (PHF) program to distinguish it from other programs that also identify with
the Housing First approach. The PHF program is built on two decades of clinical
and operational experience, manuals, fidelity standards, and research findings,
attesting to the model's effectiveness. After a 2007 peer review of these studies
and other materials, the PHF program was entered into the National Registry
of Evidence-based Programs maintained by SAMHSA, the Substance Abuse and
Mental Health Services Administration of the U.S. Department of Health and
Human Services.

Today, the PHF program has been replicated in more than one hundred cities
across the United States, and a growing number of programs are in place in Canada
and Europe. Its success has not gone unnoticed. Among its many honors, Pathways
to Housing was awarded the Excellence in Innovation Award from the National
Council for Community Behavioral Health Care, which represents 1,300 U.S. organizations that provide treatment and rehabilitation for people with mental illnesses
and addiction disorders. The PHF program also earned the American Psychiatric
Association's Gold Award, ranking it first among community mental health

programs. (A list of other awards can be found in this book's appendix E or on the Pathways Web site at www.pathwaystohousing.org.)

The PHF program is a proven, effective, cost-saving approach for both the street-dwelling homeless and those staying in shelters, jails, state hospitals, or other institutions. The problem of homelessness among adults with severe mental illness still persists, of course, but with the PHF approach, this issue can now be effectively addressed on a large scale. In June 2010, the U.S. Interagency Council on Homelessness (www.usich.gov) unveiled the federal five-year plan to end homelessness, and this plan includes Housing First as one of its five core strategies.

This manual was created after Pathways to Housing received countless inquiries from agencies and individuals wanting to replicate the successful PHF program in their own countries and communities. Written from the point of view of PHF staff, this manual describes the fundamentals of the PHF program—including the philosophy, principles, and values that guide its thought, operation, and administration. Because the needs, goals, and capabilities of each agency and potential program implementer are so varied, this manual is intended not only for readers planning to introduce the PHF model into new locations, but also for those seeking to integrate PHF's ideals into more traditional programs. Those who intend to adopt and operate a PHF program will want to seek more specific direction from qualified PHF experts on launching and operating the program.

While PHF sounds very simple and practical, it is actually a complex clinical and housing intervention. As with other complex clinical interventions, mastering this program requires practice and supervision. Because PHF is based on the principles of consumer choice and individualized treatment, it is impossible to anticipate or describe how the program will unfold for each and every client. This manual offers guidance, principles, procedures, and clinical experience as a framework. Translating these principles and procedures into day-to-day decisions based on input from each client requires training and supervised practice. Because every client makes unique choices, no two days in a PHF program are ever alike. Even if your community lacks the capacity to begin a full-scale PHF program, this manual can help you begin a practice or a small program that respects and responds to the voices of men, women, and families who want nothing more than to attain what should always be attainable: a home.

Who Should Read This Manual—and Why

This manual explains PHF practices in detail, including staffing patterns, finances, and operations. By laying bare the program, we hope that administrators, advocates, policy makers, educators, and others may find it useful for implementing (or contemplating) a PHF program in their communities. We also hope it will prove useful to researchers interested in studying particular elements of the program that account for its success. Beyond its instructional and educational purposes, we hope this manual will serve as an affirmation to those who work in traditional programs but believe in consumer-driven programs at heart. Finally, we hope that this manual will inspire the broader adoption of practices that foster client dignity and empowerment.

How to Use This Manual

Most of this book addresses the *what, why,* and *how* of the Housing First model. But it also covers the *if*—that is, if readers are ready to launch a PHF program in their own community.

Because many readers may not be familiar with the Housing First model, this book begins with a general description of the model, followed by a detailed discussion of the unique Pathways Housing First approach (chapters 1 and 2). Chapters 3 through 6 offer a nuts-and-bolts description of PHF's team approach to housing and treatment services. Chapter 7 discusses some of the other evidence-based practices integrated within the PHF program; this discussion can help readers determine whether PHF is a good fit for their agency or program. Chapter 8 offers guidance on what steps need to be taken next for those who want to go forward with a PHF program—including information on possible funding sources and other avenues of support. (You'll find a more detailed chapter overview below.)

If readers are already familiar with the precepts of Housing First and know they want to launch a PHF program, they may want to read chapter 8 first before delving into the more detailed chapters that precede it.

Chapter Overview

Chapter 1, "The Pathways Housing First Program," introduces the PHF approach, describing the origins of the model and its clinical and philosophical foundations.

Chapter 2, "Initial Program Steps," discusses the population served by PHF; it also describes how eligibility is determined, how clients are referred and engaged in the program, how housing preferences are determined, the use of interim housing, and what initial services might be needed.

Chapter 3, "Housing and Housing Support Services," discusses the program's philosophy on housing and how it practices that philosophy with clients, including the process of searching for an apartment, signing a lease, furnishing the apartment, and moving in. This chapter also covers property management issues, noting some of the PHF program's benefits for landlords, and offers solutions to some common housing challenges clients face.

Chapter 4, "An Interdisciplinary Approach: How the ACT and ICM Teams Serve Clients," describes the community-based treatment and support services offered in a PHF program. Two types of teams can work in this framework: the assertive community treatment (ACT) team (for clients with severe psychiatric disorders) and the intensive case management (ICM) team (for those with more moderate psychiatric disorders). This chapter also covers the treatment planning process and the home visit.

Chapter 5, "The PHF Assertive Community Treatment Team," details some of the ACT team's clinical operations, including staff roles and the essential daily "morning meeting" for the ACT team in a PHF setting, complete with sample schedules, other essential forms, and a hypothetical meeting outline. The weekly conference review is also briefly discussed.

Chapter 6, "The PHF Intensive Case Management Team," discusses the ICM team's strengths model approach to services and some of its operational matters in a PHF setting, such as staff roles and meeting procedures.

Chapter 7, "Incorporating Other Evidence-Based Practices," provides a broad overview of integrated dual disorders treatment (IDDT) and its core elements, which include harm reduction, Stages of Change, and Motivational Interviewing. It also addresses the principle of Wellness Management and Recovery and the Supported Employment approach. In the PHF context, ACT and ICM teams use these evidence-based practices in their client interactions and as they assist clients with recovery and community integration.

Chapter 8, "Bringing PHF to Your Community," offers guidance to prospective program implementers who, after reviewing this manual, want to take the next steps toward launching a PHF program in their area. It includes a brief discussion of possible funding sources and offers some advice on connecting and working with various governmental and not-for-profit agencies.

Each chapter ends with a summary of the key points discussed. The manual concludes with information about the Pathways Housing First Training Institute.

This manual's appendices contain reviews of the quantitative and qualitative research on the PHF program and provide the results of several cost-effectiveness studies from several cities. They also contain a sample of some of the documents and forms commonly used in PHF programs; a discussion of common administrative concerns; and a list of awards honoring Pathways to Housing and its founder, Dr. Sam Tsemberis.

Terminology

This glossary explains some terms commonly used in PHF programs.

ACT team: For clients with severe psychiatric disabilities and multiple needs, assertive community treatment teams are composed of multidisciplinary staff members who directly provide clinical and support services. The ACT team as a whole is the service provider, offering around-the-clock on-call services and maintaining a low participant-to-staff ratio.

ICM team: For moderately disabled clients, intensive case management teams are composed of clinicians or other caseworkers. ICM teams use a "caseload" practice model with a ratio of about ten to twenty participants per staff member. Staff are available on call; the PHF model recommends that one case manager be available twenty-four hours a day, seven days a week. (Many other Housing First programs offer twelve-hour coverage, perhaps using another crisis line service to implement around-the-clock on-call service.)

Client: A person receiving services in the PHF program, also referred to as *consumer, participant,* or *tenant.*

Consumer-driven (client-driven): With this approach, PHF invites its clients (consumers) to be their own decision makers—to drive the process themselves. Clients in large measure determine how housing, clinical support, and services will be delivered to them. Clients are asked for their preference in type of housing (almost all choose an apartment of their own), location, furnishings, and other personal amenities. Clients also determine the type, sequence, and intensity of services and treatment options (rather than the clinician or provider dictating these). While the PHF program offers many choices, it also has two requirements: (1) participants must agree to a weekly apartment visit by program staff, and (2) they must agree to the terms and conditions of a standard lease, including paying 30 percent of their income toward rent.

Harm reduction: This is a practical, client-directed approach that uses multiple strategies, including abstinence, to help clients manage their addictions and psychiatric symptoms. Harm reduction focuses on reducing the negative consequences of harmful behaviors related to drug and alcohol abuse or untreated psychiatric symptoms. With harm reduction, staff "meet clients where they are" and start the treatment process from there, helping them gradually gain control over their harmful behaviors.

Pathways Housing First (PHF): This term is used throughout the manual to refer to the Pathways Housing First program.

Pathways to Housing or Pathways to Housing, Inc.: This is the legal name of the not-for-profit corporation founded in 1992 in New York City by Dr. Sam Tsemberis, credited as the originator of the Housing First model and creator of the unique Pathways Housing First program.

Chapter 1

The Pathways Housing First Program

THE PATHWAYS HOUSING FIRST (PHF) PROGRAM has been replicated in more than 100 cities throughout the United States, Canada, and Europe. Of the more than 400 U.S. cities and counties with ten-year plans to end chronic homelessness, according the National Alliance to End Homelessness, 67 percent of these plans incorporate PHF as a component.

This chapter describes the PHF program's clinical and housing interventions, its wide range of recovery-oriented services, and its philosophical assumptions: the principles, beliefs, and values that guide it, from initial contact with clients to their discharge or graduation.

Why It Works

By providing a person with a home, PHF offers dignity and ignites hope in individuals who have often been treated in an undignified manner and who have felt hopeless for years. Most importantly, the transformation of moving from homelessness into a home of one's own begins the process of physical and psychological healing and immediately changes a person's status from an outcast to a valued member of the community. Clients "graduate" from the PHF program when they no longer need the program's support to maintain their own home.

Among the PHF program's proven advantages are these:

- PHF takes a client-centered approach that ends homelessness for people who have remained homeless for years. From the point of engagement, PHF empowers clients to make choices, develop self-determination, and begin their individual journeys toward recovery and community integration.

- PHF has a twenty-year track record of success. Because it results in better housing retention and treatment outcomes at significantly lower costs, it offers a more favorable return on investment than other programs.

- A PHF program has a very quick start-up time because it rents affordable apartments from the existing rental market. Moreover, it is very efficient: on average, clients can move from a homeless situation into their own apartment in two to four weeks.

- PHF eliminates the need for costly long-term shelters and transitional housing and treatment services aimed at preparing clients to become "housing ready." The average cost of running a PHF program is $15,000 to $25,000 per person per year, depending on the intensity of services needed and local housing market rents. This cost compares very favorably with the annual per-person cost of emergency room visits, jail, hospital, and shelter stays. In fact, it costs less than letting a person with multiple needs remain homeless while receiving acute care services. There are also enormous societal and quality-of-life costs for the people who remain homeless and for the general population; these are difficult to quantify.

- PHF promotes client choice and self-determination and, at the same time, encourages the use of mental health, addiction, and other services. By providing housing *first,* the program also offers the fundamental safety and security that makes it possible for clients to consider and obtain other services.

The Origins of Housing First:
An Alternative to Linear Residential Treatment

To understand why the Pathways Housing First program was developed and why it embraces the principles and practices that drive it today, it is helpful to know how other programs operate. Traditional supportive housing—or what we often refer to as "treatment as usual"—is actually a composite of several program components that have been described as a *linear residential treatment* system of care, or LRT.

The LRT or Continuum of Care services was initially established during the early 1980s, the beginning of this epoch of homelessness. The LRT sought to address the needs of people who were homeless and living on the streets, a population that clearly included a disproportionately high number of people with mental illness. With government funding, mental health agencies quickly mobilized to develop a range of programs intended to move clients along the continuum in a step-by-step manner from outreach to temporary housing, then to transitional housing, and eventually to permanent housing. The treatment philosophy underlying these Continuum of Care programs was probably based on the therapeutic milieu model used in psychiatric units—a step-by-step level system in which patients could earn privileges by complying with ward rules. The pace and potential for clients to suc-cessfully progress through this LRT system are functions of each program's rules and each client's ability to comply with the rules, which almost always means to maintain sobriety and participate in psychiatric treatment. Until the advent of Housing First, the LRT continuum was the only program model for the homeless mentally ill, and it is still widely used throughout the United States and Canada. The LRT model is not empirically based, but it is nonetheless well established and supported through steady revenue streams of government funding. For example, the U.S. Department of Housing and Urban Development (HUD) funds thousands of LRT programs through its annual Continuum of Care process.

A fully developed LRT system of care is composed of outreach teams, drop-in centers, safe havens, shelters, and several types of transitional housing with stay limits ranging from six months to two years. This approach incorporates an array of permanent supportive housing (PSH) programs, such as community residences and small and large single-room-occupancy buildings with social services on site. PSH programs can also involve some mixed-use housing, where people with psychiatric disabilities occupy about half the units of a building and the remaining tenants are people who have a variety of special needs or who are low-income community residents. Independent and shared apartments are also a component. But in the LRT model, *almost all permanent housing options, especially apartments, are available to clients only if they first demonstrate continued participation in psychiatric treatment and achieve a period of sobriety.* These requirements create insurmountable hurdles for many people with co-occurring disorders—that is, those who have psychiatric and substance use problems—causing them to remain chronically homeless.

Research shows that traditional supportive housing programs (a single-site building that bundles housing and treatment services under the same roof) face some programmatic and ethical challenges. After evaluating a number of such supportive housing programs in New York City, Lipton and his colleagues reported that bundling housing and social services can jeopardize housing stability.[10] Often, when a client living in an LRT building suffers a relapse, he or she can be evicted by the housing program, which usually means a return to homelessness plus the loss of the established and necessary social support services, because these services were located in that building. When housing and treatment are under the same roof, site-based service providers lack the capacity to provide follow-up support or treatment in another location, whether it is a hospital, the street, or another housing option in the community.

A 1999 HUD-funded study of twenty-eight traditional housing programs in Philadelphia showed that about half of residents stayed three or more years. Considered as positive outcomes, one-third of those who eventually left went to independent and other living situations. Considered as negative outcomes, two-thirds who left returned to homelessness, institutions, and unspecified locations. This latter group also had higher incidences of both severe mental illness and substance abuse and needed more support services than those who remained housed.[11]

Many researchers and program analysts have pointed out that there is potential for ethical problems in the LRT model because there is an element of coercion when housing is offered only as a reward for participation in treatment.[12] While such coercion is often justified on therapeutic, pragmatic, and even moral grounds, does it lead to greater compliance with treatment? Most mental health experts argue that it does not. In an article summarizing the literature on this subject, Michael Allen concludes that coercion violates the therapeutic alliance, violates ethical principles of mental health practitioners, and "does not work as well as programs that take a Housing First approach." [13]

This is why the PHF program was developed. We observed that many clients were unable either to gain admission to LRT programs or to retain housing once they were admitted. Others—those who had been homeless for years and had psychiatric disabilities that interfered with their thinking and perceptions—never even applied to these treatment-first housing programs.

This subgroup among those who are homeless has been more recently called the "chronically homeless." Some LRT housing providers take the position that these consumers remain homeless because of some personal failing or personality characteristic that makes them "treatment resistant" or "hard to house."

From the PHF perspective, the continued presence of the chronically homeless is evidence not of individual failures, but of failings inherent in the LRT model of care. It turns out the so-called "hard-to-house" client has a vastly different perspective than the LRT providers do. The treatment-first approach is not consistent with these clients' priorities. The urgent needs for people who are homeless are survival, safety, and security. Much of their time is consumed with fear and worry about where, when, or whether they will be able to find their next meal or a safe place to sleep; how to fend off illness, pain, and exhaustion; and efforts to avoid the attention of the police. Most clients who have been homeless for years have likely tried and failed (either voluntarily or involuntarily) on many occasions to engage in treatment in order to obtain housing. *Housing is fundamental to survival and meets the basic human needs of refuge and safety, which are primal needs for all of us.*

Thus, for people who are homeless with co-occurring disorders, treatment-first housing programs are often puzzling. Indeed, the priorities of the LRT system are almost antithetical to their own. It appears that the treatment-first model was developed from the clinician's perspective, rather than the homeless person's. In fact, the LRT model seems to be loosely based on several erroneous clinical assumptions about the capabilities of clients with co-occurring disorders, and these assumptions are found in many mental health treatment and housing programs today.

Among the LRT model's erroneous assumptions:

1. Clients must first demonstrate they can live successfully in transitional congregate housing before they can manage independent housing.

2. Clients with co-occurring psychiatric and addiction disorders must first be in psychiatric treatment and clean and sober before they can be housed.

3. Clients will value housing more if they have to earn it (housing as a privilege). In the LRT model, housing is earned by demonstrating compliance with treatment, sobriety, and following program rules.

4. Clinicians must set goals for clients because they are incapable of making choices or settings goals for themselves.

5. Clients with severe psychiatric disabilities need to live in residences with on-site staff because they require around-the-clock supervision.

Furthermore, these assumptions persist even in light of a growing body of research that indicates consumers are capable of setting their own goals and, with support, living independently without first living in transitional settings. Indeed, the evidence suggests that not only are consumers capable of making choices, they are far likelier to stay in housing programs that allow them greater choice.[14] Studies in the area of psychiatric rehabilitation indicate that the most effective way to learn the skills necessary for living independently in the community is not in a group or transitional setting invented for that purpose, but in the actual community where the skills will be practiced.

If the treatment-then-housing approach is riddled with erroneous clinical assumptions and contributes to creating chronic homelessness, why does it persist? Part of the answer lies in the enormous discrepancy between the supply and demand of affordable supportive housing. For every available supportive housing slot, there can be literally hundreds of applicants. Thus, providers can easily meet their program census targets while only selecting those applicants who have successfully met their treatment-based program requirements, which leaves many of the most vulnerable among the homeless distressed and roaming the streets.

Pathways Housing First was developed as an effective antidote to the clinician-driven approach of the LRT system—and for people like Candice.

CANDICE, A FIFTY-THREE-YEAR-OLD NATIVE NEW YORKER, was homeless for more than fifteen years when referred to Pathways. She stayed on the streets but slept in a tent she frequently pitched in an Upper West Side park. Her other campsites included the traffic median on Broadway above Seventy-second Street. Her highly visible blue tent drew immediate attention from concerned citizens, outreach teams, and the police, typically resulting in a hasty involuntary transport and admission at one of local psychiatric hospitals. A few weeks later, after her discharge, this cycle would repeat.

Because of Candice's prominent psychotic symptoms that featured paranoia and fear about government control, most outreach and other aid workers encouraged her to seek treatment. The workers knew that without treatment they could not admit her to a supportive housing program. She repeatedly and adamantly refused all psychiatric and medical treatments.

In their first meeting with Candice, Pathways staff offered to help her with anything she needed, including an apartment of her own—no strings attached. It took several visits to convince her that the housing offer was genuine, unconditional, and free of government controls. She accepted the apartment on the condition that her signature would not be required and that she be permitted to pitch her tent inside her new home.

After she moved in, staff continued to work with her and gained a better understanding of her circumstances. They learned she was employed as a nurse when she had had her first psychotic episode more than twenty years ago. As she grew more comfortable and felt safe in her home, she stopped sleeping in the tent and began sleeping on the couch in the living room, and eventually in her own bed. After years of eating canned and uncooked foods, she began to enjoy her own home-cooked meals. Her relationship with her family was transformed, with arguments about her treatment refusals replaced by enjoyable visits at holidays. Her condition has continued to improve, with only one hospitalization in the four years since she started receiving Pathways' services.

The Pathways Housing First program, which provides people like Candice immediate access to permanent independent housing—an apartment, a home of one's own, with off-site intensive services—is clearly a radical departure from past practices. This is why the PHF program created a paradigm shift in the field of housing and treatment options. Equally important, the program has expanded our view of what is considered possible for people who are homeless and suffer from mental illness and addiction disorders. The PHF program effectively ends chronic homelessness by using a fundamentally consumer-directed service approach that supports clients in pursuing their own goals by providing them with housing first.

The Principles of Housing First

It bears repeating: PHF is based on the belief that housing is a basic human right rather than something people with mental illness have to earn or prove they deserve by being in treatment. It is also based on the belief that people who are homeless and who have psychiatric disabilities are capable of defining their own goals. A fundamental principle is that consumers should have a choice in the housing and services they receive and that services should be geared toward supporting their recovery.

At Pathways, we believe in

- housing as a basic human right

- respect, warmth, and compassion for all clients

- a commitment to working with clients for as long as they need

- scattered-site housing; independent apartments

- separation of housing and services

- consumer choice and self-determination

- a recovery orientation

- harm reduction

What follows is a more detailed discussion about these beliefs, values, and principles, and how they govern the PHF approach. Overall, our purpose is to create the program equivalent of unconditional love.

Housing as a Basic Human Right

> *Everyone has the right to a standard of living adequate for the health and well-being of himself and his family, including food, clothing, housing, and medical care and necessary social services, and the right to security in the event of unemployment, sickness, disability, widowhood, old age, or other lack of livelihood in circumstances beyond his control.*

> —**Article 25(1), United Nations Declaration of Human Rights, 1948**

In the PHF program, housing is not offered as an enticement to get an individual into treatment or as coercion to get an individual to sober up. It is instead offered as a matter of right.

The PHF program has an 85 percent success rate for housing—and for *keeping* housed—people who have been homeless for years. This rate has been verified by numerous scientific and empirically sound studies conducted by a number of researchers across many programs. (See appendix A.) However, even after all the research, after years of operation, and after thousands of people have been housed, no one can predict which tenant will succeed and which one will fail. Nonetheless, in the PHF program every person who is homeless and has psychiatric disabilities or a substance abuse diagnosis is given support and a chance to succeed in an apartment of his or her own. The program does not practice screening (except to ensure that the most vulnerable are selected and admitted) and does not presume to know who will succeed.

It is for that reason that Pathways Housing First is known as a program that will move anyone, no matter the disability or addiction, into an apartment of his or her own.

Respect, Warmth, and Compassion for All Clients

> *The staff members treat us all as if we were family, and for me, that is something I will cherish for many years to come.*

> —**Pathways Housing First client**

Warmth, respect, and compassion lie at the heart of all communication between staff and clients. Although these qualities are seldom documented in chart notes, they are actually the heart and soul of the PHF program. They are the elements that create a healthy, positive, forward-looking relationship and program culture that affects clients and staff alike—and they must be present from the very beginning. A respectful, warm, barrier-free welcome is essential. When a client enters the program, the first message he or she should receive is "Welcome, Mr. [or Ms.] Jones. We are glad you are here" and "We are glad to see you."

While these qualities may seem self-evident to some clinicians, we draw particular attention to them here because it is important to understand not only the components of an intervention but the quality with which that intervention is provided. For example, most programs have an intake process that involves a staff member sitting with a client and obtaining information regarding demographics and psychosocial history. But nonverbal communication is also occurring. What is the staff member communicating on this "channel"? Is this a routine intake, or is it a respectful interview, with a warm greeting and welcome? Is this passive data collection, or is the staff member engaged, interested, and empathically responsive to the client's answers? It is important to attend to the nonverbal messages and attitudes we convey to our clients, because the most important messages—such as hope, respect, and possibility for success—are conveyed through these channels.

It bears repeating: A program culture in which client-staff interactions are based on respect, warmth, and compassion from the moment of contact to graduation from the program—this culture is a key to the health and success of the PHF program.

A Commitment to Clients

Most of the clients served by PHF programs have long histories of isolation and, paradoxically, of using multiple service providers. Once a person is accepted into a PHF program, the staff must convey a consistent message of commitment to him or her. The client must be able to say, "Pathways is committed to working with me. They will not lose track of me." Then the program staff must put in place everything needed to demonstrate this commitment. To paraphrase Jessica Benjamin's book about love, "There is no commitment; there is only *proof* of commitment."

This commitment is particularly evident during times when the client may be hospitalized, incarcerated, or, in extreme cases, returned to homelessness. The story of Mr. M. illustrates the point.

. . . .

MR. M. LIVED ON THE STREETS FOR YEARS *before entering the PHF program. He knew firsthand and all too well the discontinuity of services between outreach, psychiatric hospitals, jail, and shelters. During his years of homelessness and hunger, he often frequented soup kitchens and had even learned to pray in several languages in order to get his meals. His struggles with addiction resulted in several arrests and after each incarceration, he returned to the PHF program.*

Housed now for more than ten years, Mr. M. jokes about the stick-to-it-iveness of one of the staff: "When I went to jail that last time, it was for two years, and I thought I was finally rid of her. I wouldn't have to listen any more to her 'How ya doin'?' and 'How can I help you?' I had just about finished serving my sentence and about a month before my release, sure enough, I get a letter from her! 'Hi, Mr. M., we know you'll be released soon and we were wondering if you've given any thought to where you want to live…' There is just no getting rid of these people!" (big smile)

. . . .

Scattered-Site Housing

> *I never believed in my wildest dreams I'd find Pathways. They brought me to an apartment in the Bronx. I had such a beautiful apartment—just me—it was something really unbelievable. So I said to myself, "I'm gonna be a good citizen and help people if I can." [That was] fourteen years ago, and I've gotten a lot better, but I can still do better.*
>
> **—Pathways Housing First client**

PHF rents suitable, affordable, decent apartments from property owners in the community. Apartments are rented at fair market value and meet government housing quality standards. This housing model—known as "scattered-site independent housing"—honors clients' preferences such as choosing apartments in neighborhoods with which they are familiar. The PHF program does not own any housing. Instead, either directly or through collaboration with a housing agency, PHF obtains affordable apartments and provides a rent subsidy on its clients' behalf. (Naturally, some housing and neighborhood choices are restricted by affordability of neighborhoods and units.)

The program limits leases to no more than 20 percent of the units in any one building. (The percentage may be higher for suburban or rural clients living in small multi-family units.) This "scattered-site" feature of the housing model helps ensure that people with psychiatric disabilities are not all housed together in one building but are integrated into their buildings and into their communities. In this model, clients don't move into a ready-made unit of a housing program—they move into their own apartments in the neighborhood of their choice. Clients are quick to recognize and appreciate the enormous difference between these two approaches, and they become immediately invested in keeping the apartments and turning them into homes. They also become invested in themselves.

Enormous changes take place when clients move from being homeless to having a place of their own. People place a high value on having their own place and become highly motivated to keep it. Some people spontaneously begin to work on their sobriety and seek treatment as a way of improving their own well-being, thereby increasing their chances for successful tenure. This positive outcome is worth emphasizing for PHF, especially given how determined traditional providers are about insisting on treatment and sobriety *before* housing.

Another remarkable outcome of this scattered-site model is its commitment to social inclusion. The other tenants in the building provide a normative context for neighborly behavior that helps PHF clients participate in community living in ways that, for some, had never before been available.

This model also allows rapid start-up and ease of relocation. Because the program's housing component consists of renting apartments available on the open rental market, there is no need for lengthy project planning and construction. PHF clients can quite literally go from being homeless on the streets one day to being housed and thinking about grocery shopping and paying the rent the next day. If clients have a difficult adjustment in their first apartment, they can easily and quickly be relocated to another one while maintaining the continuity and support of their off-site mobile treatment team through the transition.

Separation of Housing and Services

> Some people think when you offer housing right away that you're actually enabling people as opposed to helping them get better. Our experience has been that providing housing first, and then treatment, actually has more effective results in reducing addiction and mental health symptoms than trying to do it the other way. The other way works for some people, but it hasn't worked for the people who are chronically homeless.
>
> —**Sam Tsemberis, founder and CEO, Pathways to Housing, Inc.**

All PHF clients have ready, reliable access to treatment and comprehensive support services, usually through a multidisciplinary team approach such as an assertive community treatment (ACT) or intensive case management (ICM) program. (See chapters 4 through 6 for details on the ACT and ICM teams.) These teams are located off-site, but they are available on call 24/7. They provide most services in a client's natural environment—usually in the apartment, neighborhood, or workplace. The service is time-unlimited; it is offered as long as a client needs the given level of support.

The aim of the support and treatment is to help clients address their needs: physical health, mental health, employment, family reconnection, recovery goals, and/or addiction problems. These clinical issues are regarded as separate and distinct from clients' housing issues—matters such as apartment maintenance, problems with paying rent, lease renewals, and so on. The criteria that determine a client's success as a tenant or a client of an ACT team are very different. For example, if a client has a psychotic episode and needs inpatient hospital treatment, she would receive help getting to the hospital and help returning to her apartment after discharge. In this example, the housing domain and clinical domain are separate; in other words, she does not risk losing her apartment because she had a clinical crisis.

She would risk losing her apartment only for the same reasons any other leaseholder in the building would: nonpayment of rent, too many visitors, illegal activity in the apartment, noise or disruption, or any other behavior that constitutes a lease violation. Even if she was evicted for one of these reasons, she would lose her apartment but, because the PHF team is off-site, she would still have the support of the team while relocating to another unit.

By separating the criteria for getting and keeping housing from a client's treatment status—while at the same time maintaining a close ongoing relationship between these two components—PHF programs help prevent the recurrence of homelessness when clients relapse into substance abuse or have a psychiatric crisis. When necessary, team members provide intensive treatment or facilitate admission to a detox center or hospital to address a clinical crisis. However, there is no need to add eviction or fear of eviction into a clinical crisis. When the crisis passes (e.g., after the client completes inpatient treatment), the client simply does what any other human being would want to do: he or she goes home.

Similarly, in the event of an eviction for a lease violation, PHF's housing staff will facilitate a move directly into another apartment if one is available. If not, housing staff will help move the client into short-term housing until another apartment can be found. This continuity is possible because the clinical team is off-site, separate from any housing component. Thus, the same team members can help the client move from one place to another. In this manner, the PHF model provides continuity of clinical care during a housing crisis, and continuity of housing stability during a clinical crisis.

There is another advantage to separating housing and clinical services. As clients continue to attain self-care skills and begin to develop supports and connections within their new communities, they will need fewer or less frequent clinical services. As a client's situation stabilizes, the team will visit the apartment less and less often. Clients can easily be transferred from ACT services to ICM services with no disruption in housing. This separation of clinical from housing services allows for flexible adjustments in frequency of services and an easy way to continue matching the client's needs to the support team's services while keeping housing constant.

When the client is self-sufficient, there can be a complete separation of housing and services. The client continues to live in the apartment and pay rent, with no need for program services. *A client does not need to move out of an apartment or transition elsewhere in order to graduate from the PHF program. Graduation simply means that PHF services are discontinued or the client receives less-intensive services through a community-based program and continues to live at home.*

Consumer Choice and Self-Determination

Twenty years ago, who would have imagined that the most humane and effective solution for ending homelessness would come directly from the people who were living on the streets—people who were, by all accounts, helpless, disoriented, and vulnerable? We first had to learn to stop letting our assumptions get in the way of listening to their needs. All we had to do was ask and listen to what they were telling us.

**—Sam Tsemberis, Ph.D., and Stephanie LeMelle, M.D.,
Pathways to Housing, Inc. Annual Report, 2007**

The remarkable success of the PHF program gives credence to the idea that people who are experiencing homelessness and who also have psychiatric disabilities are capable of defining their own recovery goals. This idea has long been resisted by traditional mental health services, but it is an idea whose time has come. A steadfast principle of PHF is that clients know what their needs are and have clear preferences about their lives and recovery. This client-directed approach is the basis of the initial engagement and guides housing and services throughout all program interactions. Stan's story illustrates that even those who are chronically homeless with psychiatric issues can prioritize their care and play a role in their treatment.

THE DAY PHF STAFF MET FIFTY-FIVE-YEAR-OLD STAN, he was sitting in front of a coffee shop in his favorite downtown neighborhood, occasionally waving or saying hello to passersby. He was charming and articulate, and the benefit of the education he had received at the prestigious university he attended at the time of his first psychotic break could still be seen. Now, having lived on the streets for decades, he was introduced to the idea of enrolling in the PHF program. Stan was tentative about accepting offers of any kind because he had been in and out of many programs before. But his health was suffering: Stan's shoes could not contain his swollen ankles, and his feet were infected and oozing pus in several areas. When staff expressed their concern for the condition of his feet, Stan agreed to be taken to the emergency room, provided that staff would accompany him though the admission process.

The emergency admissions nurse interviewed Stan about his complaints. "My feet," he told her, pointing to them, "I am in pain, considerable pain."

She looked at his feet and wrote some notes before continuing, "Any other problems or conditions?"

"Yes," he replied, "I also have schizophrenia, but that isn't bothering me so much right now."

. . . .

Most traditional supportive housing programs are highly structured and permit only a narrow range of client choices. By limiting choice, these highly structured programs discourage autonomy, and they erode the very skills recovering people need to function effectively in the community.

In sharp contrast to such programs, client self-determination drives the PHF philosophy. PHF program staff start by asking clients what they want, and they proceed by honoring the answer that so many clients give: "I want a place to live." Clients then actively work with staff to select the neighborhood where they wish to live. They choose their own apartments. They select their own furniture and household items. If they so desire, they can choose to have a roommate.

Once housed—with safety and security no longer a daily struggle—clients begin to focus on other areas of their lives. Some of these areas have long been neglected, and some represent new beginnings and new challenges. The range and variety of goals that clients, when housed, set for themselves are as diverse as the clients themselves: reconnecting with family, finding a job, treating chronic health problems, shopping for food, or just recuperating from the extreme stress of street life.

Self-determination in the PHF program means that clients are encouraged and supported in selecting which priorities to address as they begin to build the life they want.

There are some nonnegotiable requirements, however. All clients are required to meet with program staff at least once each week. The channels of communication between clients and program staff must be kept open—especially in times of relapse or crisis. Although these meetings are mandatory, client self-determination remains the touchstone of the PHF program.

Honoring client self-determination is especially important in times of difficulty, such as when clients deplete their financial resources, when a landlord threatens eviction, or when a client has relapsed into addiction. In these situations, staff must resist the impulses to control or resolve a chaotic situation. Instead, staff must make every effort to help clients explore their options during the crisis. Experiential learning, in which clients are supported as they make their own decisions and observe the results, is one of the keystones of self-sufficiency. By making their own choices during difficult circumstances, clients learn about their own decision-making process, and they become better equipped to make sound decisions in the future.

This process requires patience and a long-term commitment, because the behavior cycles for these critical events may take months to unfold, and repeated events may be necessary for the learning to occur.

A Recovery Orientation

> *The freedom they have given me... They're not controlling my life; they're helping me to better my life.*
>
> **—Pathways Housing First client**

The PHF program has long embodied a recovery orientation that is now the foundation of mental health service reform. The 2003 New Freedom Commission on Mental Health report defines recovery as "the process in which people are able to live, work, learn, and participate fully in their communities."[15] With the PHF program, recovery begins with client choice and self-determination. Clients' service plans are based not on clinical assessments of their needs, but on the clients' own treatment goals. This approach helps clients stay motivated and engaged with the team.

Because treatment compliance and sobriety are not tied to retaining housing, clients are free to discuss any symptoms or substance use honestly and openly, without fearing that they will lose their housing.

The success of this service approach depends on staff and clients developing recovery-oriented working relationships. Since staff must continually convey their belief that recovery is possible and even inevitable, it is imperative that staff be carefully selected and trained. Each staff member must carry positive messages about recovery, must convey hope, must avoid hierarchical power relationships, and must convey true caring and concern. In practice, staff members must be cognizant that while doing things *for* the client may be acceptable during the engagement or initial phase of the program, the goal is to move toward a role in which they are doing things *with* clients, and then into a role in which they teach and support clients *to do things for themselves.*

There is no better way to model and promote the concept of recovery than by including peer specialists as staff on PHF teams (see chapter 5 for details on this position). In addition, a PHF program should work to expand the variety and scope of its services and include other recovery-oriented programs, such as employment support, wellness self-management, and a comprehensive health and wellness program addressing primary care, diet, cooking, exercise, meaningful leisure, community activities, and spirituality.

But most of all, staff must heed the words of one client: "Staff should assume that every person who walks through the door has the potential for recovery. Staff should just automatically assume that recovery is possible."

Harm Reduction

> *Without Pathways, I'd be lost, living on the street, and maybe dead.*
>
> **—Pathways Housing First client**

While abstinence is a strategy that works for many people struggling with addictions, it has not proven to be effective for most people served by the PHF program. Instead, the program uses a *harm-reduction* approach—and an integrated dual disorders treatment approach—to work with clients' substance abuse and mental health issues. Harm reduction is a practical, client-directed approach that uses multiple strategies, including abstinence, to help clients manage their addictions and psychiatric symptoms. Harm reduction focuses on reducing the negative consequences of harmful behaviors related to drug and alcohol abuse, such as accumulated debts and unprotected sex. It also includes managing potentially harmful consequences of untreated psychiatric symptoms such as hospitalization. It allows the process of treatment to start "where clients are" at the time and helps them gradually gain control over harmful behaviors.

PHF programs use this strategy within the context of client-defined goals. If the client does not yet consider using drugs or drinking excessively to be a problem, the focus is not placed on stopping the substance use. Instead, the focus is placed on how drugs and alcohol may interfere with the client's goals. In the case of the often-stated goal "I want to hold on to my apartment," the team member may help a client identify the ways drug use is jeopardizing that goal. For instance, the client might note that neighbors have complained to the police about the high volume of traffic through the client's apartment and that the landlord has sent several notices threatening eviction. The client and team member could conclude that using drugs with groups of people in the apartment is problematic and could lead to eviction. The client may decide to use the apartment only for personal drug use and to socialize at other people's homes. Such a seemingly small step can give clients the experience of taking incremental control over the negative consequences of their drug use and meeting their stated goals of keeping their apartments.

In another situation, perhaps the client is spending his or her benefit checks on drugs or alcohol and is at risk of eviction for nonpayment of rent. Here, the team can offer to manage a client's Social Security check as his or her representative payee to ensure timely rent payment. Even further, the team can help the client follow a budget by providing weekly installments to the client, so that the rest of the money is not spent all at once—on drugs, for example. In some instances, the team can go with the client to shop for groceries so that the rent and groceries are taken care of before the remainder of the money is spent.

Similarly, in the case of psychiatric symptoms that manifest in harmful behaviors such as hoarding—when the client collects and stores large quantities of items to the point it becomes a health and safety hazard—team members would work with the client on his or her stated goals. Perhaps in this case the client might want to regain custody of a child or improve his or her social life. So any discussions of the hoarding issues would focus on how the clutter is a barrier to achieving these goals. In instances when the compulsive collecting leads to failing a health and safety inspection, the client will risk eviction. Then the goal immediately becomes "I want to keep my apartment," and the team members work with the client to remedy the situation.

Harm reduction is not a permanent solution, but it reduces risks associated with unhealthy or dangerous behavior. There is no one strategy or list of tried-and-true interventions. Overall, harm reduction requires ingenuity and creativity. It is highly individualized, and what works for one client may not work for another. Given that the program does not require psychiatric treatment and sobriety as a precondition for housing, this harm-reduction approach is what makes the program function as well as it does. *Harm reduction is a central philosophical approach in working with addiction and psychiatric symptoms in the PHF program.*

Chapter 1 Summary

PHF is an alternative to the traditional linear residential treatment or continuum of care: Still widely used, the continuum model moves clients in a linear manner from outreach to temporary housing, then to transitional housing, and eventually to permanent housing. Research shows that this "treatment, then housing" approach creates insurmountable barriers to housing for people with co-occurring disorders and causes them to remain chronically homeless.

PHF is scientifically proven to be more successful: The PHF program has a twenty-year track record of success. Numerous scientific studies prove that it results in better outcomes at significantly lower costs relative to other residential treatment programs.

PHF program philosophy includes these principles:

- Housing is a basic human right, rather than something the person with mental illness or an addiction has to earn by first being in psychiatric treatment or achieving sobriety.

• Providing a person a home provides dignity and ignites hope in individuals who have often been treated in an undignified manner and who have felt hopeless for years. Moving from homelessness into a home of one's own leads to physical and psychological healing and changes a person's status from outcast to a valuable member of the community.

• It is crucial to establish reciprocal, trusting relationships in which clients are treated as respected, dignified individuals who deserve warmth and compassion.

• Housing and service delivery are physically separated.

• Housing is scattered and integrated into the community.

• Services are formulated and directed by a client's self-identified goals. Clients have the right to choose, modify, or refuse services and supports at any time except for one weekly home visit with staff.

• Clients with psychiatric disabilities are not required to take medication or participate in formal treatment, nor are clients with substance use disorders mandated to pursue substance use treatment.

• The PHF program uses a harm-reduction approach.

• The PHF program embodies a recovery orientation that is now the foundation of mental health service reform.

Initial Program Steps

> In less than one year, Pathways in Philadelphia has housed
> eighty-nine men and women, some of whom have lived
> on the streets of our city and passed through system after
> system for years. The Housing First model—engage, house,
> and serve—is a tribute to human hope and compassion.
>
> —Dainette M. Mintz, Director, Office of Supportive Housing,
> City of Philadelphia

THIS CHAPTER COVERS THE INITIAL STEPS of the Pathways Housing First (PHF) program. It discusses the clients the program seeks to serve, eligibility and referral issues, the engagement process, housing preferences and the use of interim housing, and other potential initial services. It also describes the sequence in which these steps unfold, as well as some principles that underlie the staff-client interactions at each phase.

Client Demographics

The Pathways Housing First program serves adults (age eighteen and over) with psychiatric disabilities who are "chronically homeless"—a term used here to mean homeless for a year or more. Many clinical conditions are closely correlated with chronic homelessness, including mental illness, addiction, acute and chronic health problems, and occasional involvement with the criminal justice system. Moreover, about 80 percent of PHF clients have co-occurring substance abuse disorders. Ages range from nineteen to seventy-nine years, depending on location; the program's demographics will reflect the characteristics of the local homeless population. There are typically more men than women in the program, especially when the program targets people who are living on the streets.

Clients with a Multitude of Problems

Chronically homeless clients have significantly higher rates of acute and chronic health problems, including diabetes, hypertension, hepatitis C, HIV, obesity, serious oral disease, nicotine dependence, malnutrition, fungal infections of the feet and nails, poorly healed or untreated old fractures, and chronic diseases of the heart, lungs, kidneys, liver, or other organs. It is important to anticipate these needs by including primary health care staff on the PHF team or ensuring that the team has ready access to primary health care. Some teams are staffed with a part-time family nurse practitioner or an internal medicine or family practice physician.

Clients who have remained chronically homeless are very likely to have had a run-in with the police, so they typically have some criminal justice involvement, for example, outstanding warrants, probation involvement, court-ordered treatment, or a history of incarceration for problematic behaviors.

Having a multitude of problems such as ill health, active psychotic symptoms and addiction, a history of incarceration or violence, or other problematic behaviors is almost certain to disqualify a person from admission to most traditional support-ive housing programs. In contrast, people with these characteristics who are referred to the PHF program are likely to go to the top of the admissions list.

Clients with a Primary Diagnosis of Substance Abuse

The PHF program has expanded its scope to include working with people who have a primary diagnosis of substance abuse. The flexibility shown to clients with severe psychiatric disabilities does not apply in the same way to clients who do not have psychotic disorders. In general, the services provided are less intensive, community service support is used, and clients are expected to comply with the same program requirements.

Determining Eligibility

To be eligible for PHF, individuals (at a mininum) must be homeless, have a severe psychiatric disability (either active symptoms or a history of hospitalization), and express an interest in participating in the program—perhaps not initially, but over time.

In addition to meeting the clinical criteria, clients must also agree to two program requirements:

1. Payment of rent: Thirty percent of clients' monthly income (usually from a government disability payment or other benefit) will go toward rent. Even if clients do not yet receive entitlements or benefits, they are still housed after they are assessed and presumed to be eligible for benefits. In these instances, the team helps them obtain the appropriate entitlements, and the PHF program pays their share of the rent until these benefits are received.

2. Weekly visits: Clients must agree to at least one weekly apartment visit by a PHF team member. Usually clients are seen more frequently, depending on the stage of treatment. Visits are increased during times of crisis.

If the client's mental status prevents him or her from signing an initial agreement for payment of rent, PHF will enroll the client on the presumption that an agreement can be reached at a later date. Waiving the rent requirement generally results from a client's refusal to sign papers, such as an application for entitlements or a lease. For example, a client may state, "I cannot sign because I cannot accept funding from a government-funded program because I am in the process of suing the government" or "I cannot sign anything while they are watching."

In such cases, the team's weekly visit to the client's apartment is extremely important to ensure this delusional thinking does not interfere with managing the apartment or with other aspects of the client's life in the community.

These weekly visits can be adjusted but are almost never waived. Clients who are reluctant to accept the weekly visit are often the ones who need it most. Resistance to the visit may mean the client is in a crisis and avoiding the PHF team. It is during such crises that visits need to be increased, not decreased.

Referrals to PHF Programs

The original PHF program and many of its current replications focus on working with clients who are literally homeless—namely, those living on the streets, in parks, in the woods on the edge of town, in subway stations, or in other public spaces where people who are homeless frequently congregate.

Client referrals are often received from drop-in centers, soup kitchens, shelters, hospital emergency rooms, and other programs that aid those who are homeless. In recent years, the range of referrals has expanded to include people who are homeless and currently in long-term psychiatric hospitals or who are incarcerated. PHF also receives referrals from mental health courts that use the PHF program as an alternative to incarceration. A small number of clients are self-referred, and others are referred from other housing agencies, by relatives, or through other sources.

The source of the referral determines how the staff initially contacts the client. If a client is currently on the streets, an outreach team may introduce the client to the program's staff and services, or PHF staff will do the outreach to meet the client.

PHF staff need to be resourceful when trying to find people who are still living on the street and who have been referred by homeless service providers and community agencies. It may be necessary to seek help from the police, family members, or other homeless people in the area.

Many communities have informal networks of homeless service providers that include the above-listed types of programs. PHF programs can work with these networks to identify people who have remained homeless for years and continue to use the local acute care and homeless services programs. Often labeled "frequent users," they exhibit the complex psychiatric, addiction, and health symptoms that make them ideal candidates for the PHF program.

When such potential clients are in a hospital, jail, or other institutional setting, PHF staff members usually engage them while they are still institutionalized. Even in that setting, these clients can be enrolled into the PHF program and then can move directly into an apartment upon discharge or release.

The Engagement Process

In the twenty-five years I've been fighting against homelessness and for affordable housing, I have never encountered an approach that is as sensible, as humane, and as effective in ending homelessness as the Housing First model pioneered by Pathways to Housing.

—Michael Allen, Pathways DC board chair

Engagement is one of the most important phases of the PHF program, because it is during these initial conversations that prospective clients develop their first impression of the program. Engagement is where the rubber meets the road; PHF's philosophical and clinical ideals are put into practice in the initial encounter. In engagement, staff members demonstrate how they listen with respect and compassion, and they set the stage so clients know what to expect from the program. It is only through effective engagement that clients who have remained homeless and disengaged for years will agree to work with the program.

Four key principles contribute to the success of the PHF engagement process:

1. Accepting the client's priority for housing (some clinicians have termed this a "radical acceptance of the client's point of view").

2. Designing services to be flexible enough to meet the client's priorities (usually it's housing *first,* but if a different priority is stated, then that's what's provided).

3. Removing obstacles whenever possible so that clients can realize their stated goal (e.g., not requiring psychiatric treatment or sobriety in order to get and keep housing).

4. Taking responsibility for follow-up by ensuring that all clients receive the services they seek (directly or via referral) in the sequence in which they seek them.

An Example of Effective Engagement

The following account by Hilary Melton, the program director at Pathways in Vermont, shows what can happen when PHF staff use the four engagement principles just described.

Melton demonstrates a respectful and accepting attitude toward her client, Henry. She does not challenge Henry's suspicions but patiently waits to find ways to eliminate the barriers to his goal: visiting the Social Security office to complete the application for the benefits he'd need to pay his portion of the rent. She manages to help Henry navigate a complex bureaucracy in a way that does not contradict his belief system. Indeed, Henry is beginning to trust Melton and the team even without ever saying as much. His follow-up request for assistance with his medical problem shows that he is starting to believe that she and the team will honor his wishes on his own terms.

> *I MET HENRY AT A LAUNDROMAT IN MONTPELIER. Henry lives in a tent right through the Vermont winter. He rides a bike, he is good with his hands, he does carpentry work, and he is very helpful around the drop-in shelter, where he builds shelves and takes out the garbage.*
>
> *A conversation with Henry is familiar to any of us who have been working with folks who, for whatever reason or whatever label, have stayed stuck in an existence of eating meals out of church basements, planning their day around where they can use a public toilet, and sleeping in a tent, a doorway, or an alley. When Henry speaks, you enter a world through his stream of seemingly incoherent words— a world full of violent images: corpses, murders, rapes, persecution, and blood.*
>
> *Yesterday, Henry—who has no identification and can name a hundred reasons why he shouldn't and can't go into the Social Security office (reasons all having to do with conspiracy, death, or torture)—went with me into the Social Security office and took the first step to getting an ID so that he can fill out an application for a housing voucher. After visiting the Social Security office, he told me that his feet hurt, that he had to remove "all of the calluses myself." He said he is in pain and wondered if he could meet our nurse.*

The reason mental health systems exist, the reason thousands or hundreds of thousands of people are in graduate schools right now getting degrees in psychiatry, or social work, or nursing, is because everyone wants to help someone like Henry.

The mental health system, as it is, isn't accessible to Henry—or to thousands of others. What are we doing wrong? Imagine a hungry person with a wallet full of money standing outside a restaurant but not going inside. The restaurant owner is changing his window display, he is offering specials, he is pumping the smell of fresh bread outside, and still the hungry person with the wallet full of cash won't come inside.

That is what is happening with our mental health system of care and the people who need it the most.

Housing First: A Critical Engagement Tool

For a person who is homeless, the offer of a place of his or her own is an enormous and spectacularly attractive incentive to enroll in the PHF program, but accepting such an offer requires effective engagement. The relationship established during engagement becomes the vehicle through which all the program's goods and services are negotiated.

The clients sought out by the program understand all too well what it means to try to scrape by for an entire month on the modest income from a benefits or disability check. In the current climate of economic crises and dwindling resources, some clients understand and appreciate that what they are being offered by PHF is the equivalent of winning a small lottery. They are not just getting an apartment of their own; they are getting the support necessary to find and rent the apartment *they* choose with furnishings *they* select. For many, this is an offer they cannot refuse. For a surprising number of others, it is an offer they initially cannot believe.

In some instances, this initial disbelief may be linked to clinical problems, and the PHF team may need more time to establish credibility. But some clients' incredulousness is based on years of experience working with other housing programs in which housing was always promised but never delivered. Unfortunately, it is a rather common practice for programs to entice people who are homeless and mentally ill into their programs by saying "come work with us for a while, and we will get you housing." Clients discover all too soon that there is no readily available housing. In fact, housing is not an option until the client agrees to take medication, participate in psychiatric treatment, and complete a long period of sobriety. It is difficult to imagine a person like Henry agreeing to see a psychiatrist and take medication as a first step to program participation.

Offering housing as leverage or coercion to get people who are homeless with psychiatric disabilities into treatment presents several ethical and clinical problems. First, the offer is misleading and disingenuous and, therefore, not an ethical way to begin a therapeutic relationship. It can have adverse effects for those clients who repeatedly try and fail to obtain housing this way. They may blame themselves for the failure and become depressed, demoralized, cynical, and hopeless. In many instances, clients served by PHF have repeatedly tried and failed in the treatment-first approach and have remained homeless. It is not surprising that upon engagement these clients may initially be reluctant to accept the word of any provider. If the prospective client's doubt persists, it may be helpful to introduce him or her to another PHF client who initially had doubts and is now enrolled in the program.

Even taking difficult cases into account, the offer of *immediate* access to housing on the client's own terms is certainly a very powerful engagement tool.

Some Basic Rules of Engagement

> Soon, Henry will not be living on the street anymore. And that is a good thing. But what Pathways does and keeps doing is bigger than that.
>
> —Hilary Melton, Program Director, Pathways Vermont

The goal of engagement is to connect and establish a relationship with the client. PHF staff need to create the conditions in which a client can feel accepted, safe, and able to express his or her point of view, as well as his or her needs and wishes. During engagement and throughout the duration of a client's time at PHF, staff members stay true to the PHF philosophy by conveying respect and compassion and by emphasizing client choice and self-determination.

The general philosophy and practice of traditional mental health care systems, at the core, is to tell clients, "This is what you *need* to do." In stark contrast, PHF continually asks, "How can we help?" and then listens to the answers. PHF service plans, which are the road map for providing services, are based on that question "How can we help?" being asked over and over about various aspects of a client's life: housing, health, wellness, vocation, interpersonal relationships, and community involvements.

In the prior example, Hilary Melton asked Henry, "How can we help?" and Henry said, "I could use an apartment"—the answer that people in the most vulnerable situations most often give. That is how engagement begins. Whether the answer is "I want a place to live," or "I want a job," or "I want to sue the government," or "I want Internet access," staff keep asking, "How can we help?" Then they listen attentively and respectfully to the answers and use the information to determine what services they need to provide.

The initial meeting

The first meeting takes place wherever the client chooses, whether it is on a park bench or at a coffee shop. Such settings establish a pattern right away: in the PHF program, important business meetings can take place in a community setting selected by the client. PHF is, after all, a *community* mental health program, not a clinic or office-based model, so most of its work takes place in the client's home or community.

The team must be very flexible with their schedule because it is difficult to predict when or where a client may show up. The team lets the client set the pace of the meeting (duration, content, and so on) and follows alongside, attentive but not intrusive or overbearing, ready to step in and provide help when asked or take the lead when needed.

In most PHF programs, it is usually the team leader, together with the program's housing specialist, who conducts the initial interview. As the client becomes more comfortable with program staff, he or she will gradually be introduced to other members of the ACT or ICM team and to the community of providers who work with the program. *In all cases, the client dictates the pace of engagement with team members.*

In the initial meeting, the team members usually learn a little of the client's history and current circumstances and then describe to the prospective client some of the services the program offers. They emphasize exactly how PHF differs from other housing and mental health or substance abuse programs in the client's past, because some clients have heard many similar descriptions before. During this initial meeting, the team members ask the client what he or she wants, and then they work to provide these things as quickly as possible. More than 90 percent of the time, the first thing PHF clients want is "a place to live," which soon translates to an apartment of their own.

The pace of engagement

Although team members make every effort to move clients directly from the streets (or other settings) into their own apartments as soon as possible, the engagement process can sometimes take a while. When this is the case, clients who have experienced trauma or are prone to paranoia may distrust staff invitations to join the program. If this occurs, staff members must stay patient, reassuring, and accepting, and they must also remain consistent in their message of offering help, hope, and possibility. However, in a small percentage of cases, the client may take many weeks or even months before trusting the staff enough to accept an apartment. Staff must be prepared for that possibility, and they must maintain a high tolerance for rejection.

For example, there are times during engagement when even a simple request to sign an agreement or document may evoke suspicion or outright refusal. When this occurs, it is important to remember that, even though the program has clear rules about its processes and operations, the objective is to successfully engage the client—not to rigidly follow the program rules. Program needs or requests must be carefully balanced with the comfort level or capability of each client. Staff must learn to allow some flexibility in applying the rules. In the case of a refusal to provide a signature, for example, one option would be to obtain approval from a PHF supervisor so that the team can immediately provide housing, then secure the client's signature for needed documents at a later date.

The clinical and legal limits of client choice

On occasion, a PHF team concludes that a client constitutes a danger to himself or herself or to others. The clinical and legal criteria for involuntary hospitalization are clearly spelled out, and the procedures for hospitalization vary from place to place. But even in these extreme circumstances, the PHF team will continue to work with the client through the crisis, hospitalization, and hospital discharge. The crisis and hospitalization are not disruptions in the process, nor a termination—they are stressful events, in the course of a long-term relationship.

Staff safety is essential in community-based work. Staff work day and night hours, and they sometimes encounter unexpected situations during what may be thought to be a routine home visit. Safety training should be a basic component of all staff education. Ultimately, if staff feel unsafe at any time, they should not continue to engage a client but immediately discontinue the conversation and seek the advice of a supervisor.

Preparing for the Apartment Search

I received a call saying, "We found an apartment for you."
I was expecting—you know—a room. But I came right in to
an apartment. Furnished. A TV—you name it. It is a miracle
to have a stove, pots and pans. . .

—Pathways Housing First client

One key part of the initial intake process involves determining the client's housing preferences. This is accomplished during the interview, when the client completes a housing preferences form that covers neighborhood location preferences, whether the ground floor or an upper floor is preferred, whether any special accommodations are needed (such as grab bars in the bathroom), and other matters that will enable staff to help the client adjust to the new unit. Often both the housing specialist (the staff person responsible for locating units) and a clinical staff member meet the client to discuss housing preferences. This information guides the search for the unit.

Clients are informed that once it is found, they will be shown the unit to ensure it is acceptable to them before they commit to signing a lease. They are also informed that the unit will be furnished and they get to select the furniture, and they are given information concerning utilities and other lease and rent-related issues.

Clients are provided with an estimated timetable for completing these activities: finding a unit, meeting the landlord, signing a lease, ordering furniture, and completing all the other steps between intake and the move-in date. This time frame explains the process and helps clients manage their expectations about it. In general, the entire process takes between two and four weeks.

Landlords sometimes request interviews with prospective tenants. In these cases, the staff prepares the client by posing possible questions and reviewing the kinds of information the client may or may not wish to disclose to the landlord.

Finding a safe, affordable apartment typically takes about two weeks, and clients are assured that they do not have to take the first one they are shown. They are told they will be shown two or three from which to choose, but more often than not, clients select the first unit they are shown.

While they wait for their apartment to be located, prepared, and furnished, clients are offered interim housing in a safe place, such as a local hotel, YMCA, YWCA, or other temporary location. The PHF program must plan and budget for this function, as well as develop a network of local interim housing providers that rent units by the day or week and are willing and able to accept PHF clients as tenants. (See chapter 3 for more details regarding interim housing.)

Initial and Ongoing Services

Determining what initial services a client will request begins with the same "How can we help you?" approach. While the answer—"a place to stay"—is very predictable when the question is first posed, the answers can be surprising when it is asked a second time. Some clients like Henry request assistance with their medical problems, while others may want help connecting with family members or addressing their addiction issues. Once staff members have a clear understanding of the client's needs and priorities, they work with the client to develop a service plan.

As with most services offered by PHF, the client directs and guides the sequence and intensity of services. The initial plan most often includes a statement of the client's immediate goals and needs to ensure that basic goods are being provided and basic survival needs are met. Later in the process, the staff and client develop a comprehensive service plan to address a client's additional needs. Developing this plan may take just two meetings for some clients, several weeks for others. The services offered typically include health and mental health treatment, family connections, addiction treatment, employment counseling, spirituality resources, legal help, information regarding benefits and entitlements, and recreation and leisure.

After a client moves into his or her apartment, he or she develops a sense of safety and security. As the client's comfort level grows, staff conversation and engagement delve deeper to include topics such as psychiatric symptoms, hospitalizations, addictions, health issues, trauma, abuse, family ties, and other areas of concern and vulnerability. By asking about and listening to a client's goals and desires, staff members can continue to engage the person, build trust, and address these issues in the context of a positive therapeutic relationship built on mutual understanding and partnership. Given the number and severity of issues that most clients face, there is a need for long-term treatment and support.

Chapter 2 Summary

Vulnerable populations: The PHF program selects clients who are homeless, have severe mental illnesses or other disabling conditions, and often have substance use issues. Clients have either been unable to gain access to traditional services, or traditional services have not proven effective for them.

Engagement: The engagement process is crucial. PHF staff must accept the client's point of view, help the client design an effective treatment program around that point of view, patiently remove obstacles that prevent clients from achieving their goals, and provide ongoing follow-up. The key question at every stage of the process is "How can I help?"

No "housing readiness" requirement: Clients have access to housing (interim and permanent) with no requirements to demonstrate readiness. This is a powerful incentive to enroll in the program.

No clinical contingencies for tenancy: Tenancy is not linked in any way with clients' adherence to clinical provisions. No requirements are placed on clients other than the expectations that they adhere to a standard lease and see staff for a face-to-face visit once a week.

Chapter 3

Housing and Housing Support Services

Thank you for saving my life. Thank you for allowing me to be a father to my children and for having a place for them to come and visit me. Thank you for the longest period without going to the hospital since I can remember. Thank you for my sobriety. Thank you for having a place to shower, a stove to cook on, a bed to sleep in, a warm place to go when it's cold. Thank you for not having to take my possessions with me everywhere I go. Thank you for my home.

—Pathways Housing First client

THIS CHAPTER OUTLINES THE HOUSING and housing support services of the Pathways Housing First program. It discusses the program's philosophy on housing and how it puts that philosophy into practice. It also outlines the client-centered process of finding, leasing, and furnishing apartments and assisting with move-in; benefits to landlords are also discussed. The chapter also covers property management issues and solutions to some common housing challenges faced by clients.

Why Housing First?

> *I could barely think. I didn't know where I was laying my head. It was too late by the time I got mental health treatment. I ended up getting locked up in the hospital. They wouldn't let me out. . . .The next thing I knew there was ca-clang, ca-clang—all these doors locking behind me and no way out.*
>
> **—Pathways Housing First client**

Housing stops the dehumanizing, expensive cycle of shuttling into and out of public institutions and short-stay, acute care settings. Pathways Housing First is a logical, humane, and cost-effective housing program.

Providing people with a safe, decent, affordable place to live gives them the opportunity to relax their vigilance, to rest comfortably, and to plan a sequence of daily events according to their own needs or priorities.

When people first enter the PHF program, they invariably ask for a safe and secure place to live, eat, and sleep; they need a place for friends and family to visit, a place of privacy away from public scrutiny. Having somewhere to live, to call one's own, is a basic human necessity, the foundation from which a person can begin to attend to mental and physical health.

The Two Program Requirements

As noted earlier, PHF clients agree to two requirements: (1) a weekly home visit from program staff, and (2) the lease and rental payment agreements. Let's examine these in more detail.

The Weekly Home Visit Requirement: Focus on Housing Issues

> *The home visit is the heart and soul of the work we do.*
>
> **—Adam Fussaro, Pathways to Housing Philadelphia**

The home visit serves many purposes, which fall into two areas: housing-related issues and more personal, clinical issues. The clinical aspect of the visit is discussed in chapter 6; here, let's focus on the home visit from a housing or property management perspective.

As they enter, the staff conducting the home visit must respect the client's rights to privacy as a tenant and honor the sanctity of each client's home. Staff members must make appointments to schedule a visit, and they do not enter a client's apartment without permission or invitation (except in an emergency). When visiting with a client, staffers are mindful that they are guests in the client's home. Although they are guests, *the home visit is truly a requirement that must not be waived,* because of its many valuable functions. After a time, when PHF program staff and client agree, the frequency of visits can be reduced.

One function of the visit is for staff to ensure that the apartment is in good shape and maintained well and that everything is in working condition. During the home visit, staff also gain insight on what support clients may need to meet their responsibilities as tenants and successfully maintain their apartments. For example, some clients may need to learn about household maintenance, grocery shopping, cooking, storing their belongings (or limiting belongings to the space available), or seeking help from the landlord or the building's management staff. Others may need help with paying the rent or budgeting. The data obtained during the visit creates the opportunity to address these issues.

Serious problems arise when newly housed clients find it difficult to balance maintaining the safety, security, and privacy that their new home affords against the urgent requests from old friends—who may still live on the streets—to stay under their roof. Under the terms of the lease, tenants have the right to have guests. But problems emerge when one guest turns into several guests, or when guests overstay their welcome and become additional tenants. When a guest is essentially living in the unit but the client does not choose to include the guest on the lease, the client faces a lease violation and may be at risk for eviction. The home visit is a very efficient and effective way to observe many situations as they develop and, ideally, intervene before the problem becomes a crisis.

The Lease Requirement

The second requirement of the program is that *clients must sign a lease* (or sublease or Use and Occupancy Agreement). They must abide by the terms and conditions of a standard lease, which includes paying 30 percent of their income toward the rent. For clients who have a disability, this is 30 percent of any entitlement, such as the United States' Supplemental Security Income (SSI) or Social Security Disability Income (SSDI) programs or Canada's Assured Income for the Severely Handicapped (AISH). Other benefits such as welfare may also play a role. If a client does not have entitlements or benefits in place, the PHF program may be able to provide housing based on the assumption that the client will later be found eligible for such entitlement.

As for clients with no source of income, the program must anticipate that it will serve a small number of clients who cannot contribute to the rent and include that calculation into its budget so that the program can pay fully for the rent.

First Steps to Securing Housing

> *I try to pick the apartment with the client—some place where they're going to be happy and walk around and feel safe and feel good and feel like, "Yes, I can be here. I can do this. I can start my life here."*
>
> **—Linda Parrish, intake coordinator, Pathways to Housing**

Housing is typically the first service provided to PHF clients, because almost every person admitted to the program places housing at the top of the list: it is their primary and most urgent need.

Clients are active decision-makers in the housing selection process. When units are located, clients are presented with a number of apartment options, and they make the final choice. In some rare instances, after considering an independent apartment, clients may decide they prefer another more social housing option or a housing program with services on site. In those instances, the PHF team assists in finding such a placement. However, the vast majority of PHF clients (more than 95 percent) prefer independent apartments of their own within the community.

The discussion of the client's housing preferences begins during the initial intake interview. Typically, the client meets with the staff member responsible for housing (the housing specialist) and a clinical staffer conducting the clinical intake interview. They describe the PHF program to the client and also explain how the housing process works.

Exploring the client's housing preferences entails a wide-ranging conversation about the client's preferred location or neighborhood; apartment type (studio or one-bedroom, ground or upper floor, front or back, and so forth); and the importance of proximity to public transportation, relatives, programs, places of worship, or other important dimensions of neighborhood. This information helps housing staff focus their search for a good fit. It is our experience, and research has shown, that a greater likelihood of success exists when clients are actively involved in selecting their own housing. Naturally, choices must be guided by the realities of the rental market.

Use of Interim Housing

This program component is recommended when working with clients who are literally homeless and staying on the streets or in parks, train stations, or other public places. Interim housing is also useful when the referring institution is a jail or prison and the client is about to be released.

Ideally, immediately after the client agrees to enroll in the PHF program, its ACT or ICM team is prepared to take steps and help the client exit from homelessness that same day. This can be easily done if the program has an established relationship with a local YMCA/YWCA, motel, or other short-term housing setting and can pay for the client to stay there until an apartment is secured. This type of interim housing has several advantages:

- The client gets some rest and begins to feel better.

- Team members gain the client's confidence as it becomes clear that this PHF program can make things happen.

- Team members are viewed as trustworthy because they are true to their word.

- The client begins to believe that things might really change.

- Team members can easily locate the client the next day for efficient follow-up.

During this interim period, team members meet frequently with the new client to ensure that day-to-day needs are met. They address health issues; apply for benefits, identifications, or other needed documents; clear outstanding warrants or other legal issues; and attend to the many other matters that need to be addressed given the enormity of the impending transition. While preparing for move-in day, their discussions and activities usually focus on plans and expectations about the new place, choosing and purchasing furniture, connecting utilities, safety, neighborhood amenities, shopping, transportation, people that clients need to contact, and clients' concern about those left behind.

Still, interim housing is not an essential component of the program, and it may not be necessary if the client is referred from an institution such as a psychiatric hospital or shelter. In these instances, it is possible to enroll the client into the program and begin the search for an apartment. The client can leave the institution with the PHF team, see and choose an apartment, and return to stay in the institution briefly while the unit is prepared.

Criteria for Choosing an Apartment

Searching for apartments is an exciting, busy time for the team and client. There is much to discuss, and the client and team meet frequently during this time. Conversations about clients' preferences are constantly reviewed and weighed against market realities, availability of units in specific neighborhoods, and the client's patience with the search.

If the program has anticipated an intake and already has a vacant apartment available for immediate occupancy, clients can move in as soon as two weeks from the initial housing meeting if they feel ready to do so.

Typically, clients are informed that they will be shown a number of units and that they can select the one they like best. In practice, this number usually does not go beyond three, and most clients, like eager adoptive parents, tend to fall in love with the first apartment they are shown.

Affordability and Amenities

> *An apartment of one's own in a regular building in the community—this model, the scattered-site apartment model—is the number one choice of consumers.*
>
> **—Harry May, Pathways NYC housing director**

For PHF apartment searches, the degree of choice is constrained by the economic realities of the rental markets and rent stipends paid by government funding. This usually limits a search to lower-middle-class neighborhoods, where the government stipend combined with the client's 30 percent contribution allows the rental of decent affordable units. In some cases, the utilities are included in the rent; in others, utilities are paid for by the PHF program or the client. All clients are required to have a telephone.

After paying 30 percent of their income toward rent, clients can choose how they want to spend the remainder of their entitlement (with SSI, about $400 a month). This is a very desirable arrangement when compared to some housing programs that may provide meals but leave clients with little or no discretionary income.

The PHF program makes every effort to find apartments in neighborhoods with relatively easy access to shops, services, and public transportation. It also tries to honor the client's preferences for neighborhood ethnicity, race, or culture. Paying attention to creating a good fit regarding client preferences, apartment, and neighborhood increases the likelihood of satisfaction and success in housing and other services.

Social Inclusion and Community Integration

Pathways Housing First seeks to help clients integrate into their community as fully as possible, and the housing component plays an important role in achieving this goal. Clients' apartments are indistinguishable from any other unit in that building and in that neighborhood. They are not identified as "mental health housing" for people with special needs or otherwise set apart from the community standard.

Such community integration is accomplished by using a "scattered-site" approach. This term probably evolved to distinguish this model from single-site programs where all the people with psychiatric disabilities live all together in a group home, community residence, or renovated building with social services on site. In the scattered-site model, the apartments are seamlessly integrated into regular buildings and communities where affordable housing is available.

The PHF program does not rent more than 20 percent of the units in any one building. For example, in a twenty-unit building, no more than four are PHF units, and PHF clients are likely to be dispersed across many blocks in a neighborhood. In communities where apartment buildings are small, however, or where the housing stock is mostly multiple-family units, this percentage must be increased. What is important here is not the absolute percentage or number of apartments, but the program's commitment to the principle of providing socially integrated housing.

The scattered-site model allows clients to live in normal community settings. The likelihood of stigma associated with being a member of a psychiatric treatment program is reduced, because the program is not visible on site, and clients live in normal settings. Clients frequently interact with their neighbors at the local market, laundromat, movie theater, coffee shop, or park. The clients share the same community and socialization opportunities as their nondisabled neighbors. Clients soon discover that being a lease-holding apartment renter, decorating their own place, and living life on their own schedule is an enormous boost to one's autonomy, self-determination, mental health, and dignity.

Housing Quality Standards

All apartments rented by the PHF client or program must be in good condition. Units must pass the equivalent of a governmental housing quality standards inspection (see appendix C-3 for a sample Apartment Readiness Checklist). Before a client's move-in date, the housing staff conducts a room-by-room inspection to make sure the unit is in move-in condition. Using the Apartment Readiness Checklist, the staff member examines doors, windows, locks, paint, floors, walls, electrical wiring and outlets, lights and light switches, plumbing, sinks, and toilet, and he or she ensures that the refrigerator and stove are functional. The staff member rates all of these items and their respective conditions, and suggests any needed improvements or repairs. If the housing staff determines that repairs are needed before the client moves in, the landlord is alerted and a meeting is scheduled to ensure these repairs have been made before the unit is occupied. The client moves in only after the apartment has satisfactorily passed the program's inspection.

Leasing or Subleasing through PHF

After a client chooses an apartment and it has been inspected, the client meets with the building manager or landlord to sign the lease. A number of people may be present at this meeting, depending on whether an outside housing agency is representing the landlord and whether the PHF program is signing or co-signing the lease. At the meeting, the PHF clinical team member is present as the client's advocate. This staffer may need to explain the terms and conditions of the lease, tenant responsibilities, rent payment, and other relevant business. As with any lease, it is a legal contract detailing the rights and responsibilities of the tenant and the landlord. In instances when the PHF program is signing the lease and subsequently renting the unit to the client (known as a *sublease, master lease,* or *head lease* arrangement), a PHF housing staffer is also present to sign the lease with the landlord and to sign a sublease with the client, ensuring that the client has the same rights and responsibilities as other tenants.

The preferred rental arrangement is for the client to sign a lease directly with the landlord. However, the program often obtains leases that name the PHF agency itself as the lessee. Such leases are often preferred by landlords who are cautious and reluctant to sign a lease with a tenant who has no housing history or landlord references, no current employment, and a poor or nonexistent credit history. In these cases, an authorized PHF representative either signs the lease as the primary tenant or co-signs the lease as the guarantor for the client.

When the PHF program serves as the leaseholder, it offers a practical and effective means of reassuring landlords and allowing the program to lease apartments for people who would not, under normal circumstances, qualify to rent them on their own. Many landlords feel more secure having the program sign a lease and guarantee the rent and damage deposit. While master leasing or head leasing is less desirable in terms of tenants' rights, this method has several operational advantages for the program. For example, it makes the housing search and leasing process more efficient, because apartments can be leased and made tenant-ready very quickly. These "ready units" can be offered as an option to a newly admitted client, and, if the unit is acceptable, the client's move-in process can be greatly expedited.

Such units are especially helpful when housing clients are discharged from the hospital or released from jail and are preparing to return to or enter the program. They are also useful for tenants who must leave an apartment before the lease's expiration date. Since the PHF program is the primary tenant on a lease, when one client has to leave an apartment, there is usually another ready to occupy it.

Finally, master leasing or head leasing eliminates some of the paperwork that would otherwise be associated with relocating clients—terminating one lease and entering into another. However, while the practice is useful for short-term efficiencies, the long-term objective of the PHF program is for each client to eventually hold his or her own lease. This goal is easier to realize after a year or two of satisfactory tenancy, when the tenant who was initially seen as unreliable is now seen as reliable by the landlord.

Use and Occupancy Agreement

Whether the client signs his or her own lease or the PHF program is named as the tenant, a Use and Occupancy Agreement should always be signed at the same time. This document describes the duties and responsibilities of the PHF program and the client. The Use and Occupancy Agreement is very similar to a standard sublease, but it also includes the agreement to once-a-week staff visits and the client's responsibility to pay 30 percent of his or her income toward rent.

The tenant retains a copy of all signed leases and agreements, as does the PHF program. Agreements should be maintained by the program and should be reviewed and updated on a regular basis.

Tenant Responsibilities and Rights

PHF believes that housing is a basic right for all people: during the engagement process, clients learn that the PHF program takes this idea seriously. As new tenants, clients now learn that with this right come certain legal and financial responsibilities as defined by their tenant agreement and lease. They also have new obligations in their roles as neighbors and community members. For example, when a client moves into an apartment, he or she becomes a member of that building and surrounding community and is expected to adhere to the same good-neighbor standards that govern any other tenant in regard to noise levels, cleanliness, and general rules about community social behavior. In the meeting in which the lease and the Use and

Occupancy Agreement are signed, clients are informed of some of the community (and lease) obligations that will affect their day-to-day interactions with the building manager or landlord, neighbors, and public service personnel.

Staffers must always remember that the transition from homelessness is not merely about exercising rights or obeying rules. They must remain sensitive to the possibility that new tenants, who may have had long histories of living on the streets or in noisy drop-in centers or shelters, face challenges in adapting to life in a quiet apartment within a community. The team must work closely with each client to facilitate this transition. During this initial period, a visit every day or every other day is common because there is much to do while setting up the apartment and getting to know the landlord and the new neighborhood.

Security and Safety Issues: The Basics

PHF staff instruct all new tenants in the use of the emergency on-call system, as well as how to reach the fire department, police, and hospital in their neighborhood. Some tenants may need instruction on the use of appliances, telephones, voice mail, intercoms, and how to exit the apartment in case of fire.

Staff hours are usually nine to five, but in the PHF program, one ACT or ICM team member is always available on call by cell phone twenty-four hours a day, seven days a week to provide assistance or manage a crisis, to help resolve a conflict, to provide friendly advice, or just to provide some light conversation during a lonely time. Staff members rotate on-call duties regularly.

Keys

> *I walked around for years without a single key: a key to a car, a key to a house, a key to anything. . . I don't think people understand what a key typifies. It's something that belongs to you. It's something huge.*
>
> **—Pathways Housing First client**

There should be three sets of keys for each apartment: one for the client, one for the support services team, and one for the housing staff. Each set should include a mailbox key. There are innumerable instances when spare sets of keys may be needed. Clients may lose their keys. With the spare set, the team can open the unit and avoid the high cost of a call to the locksmith. Access may also be necessary if a client is hospitalized or arrested and needs items from the apartment or if the PHF team needs to look after the client's pets, plants, and so on (see more on the topic of pets later in this chapter).

Staff should make it clear to clients that the duplicate keys in the staff's possession exist only to assist the client. Clients should be assured that the PHF team or housing staff will not enter without permission unless there is an emergency.

Making a Home: Physical and Emotional Comfort

Some people are still in their place after a month, and what you see is the furniture that they moved in with. . . There's nothing else in there—no personal effects—and some people will live like that for a while. There are others who will move in right away and want to make it more of a home by putting pictures up and having personal effects around.

—Ben Henwood, Pathways to Housing Philadelphia

Once the apartment is rented, there is a flurry of PHF team and client activity that includes shopping for furniture and household items, learning about the apartment and the building, and exploring neighborhood stores and other amenities. Most people involved find this to be the honeymoon period of the program, filled with a mixture of relief and joy as clients move into a place they can call home.

It is essential that apartments be furnished before clients move in. Ideally, furniture should be new and selected by the client. PHF programs must budget for these items as part of start-up costs. Once a client decides on an apartment, he or she meets with the PHF intake or housing staff to select furniture. The PHF program should have an existing relationship with a local furniture company that can offer reasonably priced furniture that is durable yet comfortable and can be delivered on short notice. One convenient way to manage the process is to have a limited catalogue of available furniture. This saves additional trips to stores where clients may see many new things they like but cannot afford.

The typical start-up furniture package includes these items:

- bed

- bureau or dresser

- sofa

- coffee table

- television set

- kitchen table

- kitchen chairs

- pots, pans, dishes, and utensils

It is critical that all apartments are equipped with telephones or that each client has a working cell phone.

Usually on moving day, a PHF staff member goes shopping with the client to purchase all the necessary household and personal items, such as sheets, blankets, pillows, towels, shower curtain, and cleaning and laundry supplies. The PHF program also provides assistance and funds for at least one week's worth of groceries upon move-in.

As a step toward easing into their homes, clients can choose to partake in as many of the moving-in activities as they wish. For most clients, this is the first time in years that they have lived independently in an apartment, so calling the electric company, for example, to provide the address and name that will appear on the bill can be an empowering experience. For others, this activity may be too overwhelming.

In Canada, most utility and phone companies require a deposit or a reference from a former landlord. This can be quite difficult, or even impossible, for some clients to get. One way to handle this issue is for PHF program staff to set up the account and bill the client for the costs.

In every aspect of this process—from the initial discussion about housing preferences to moving day and every day thereafter—PHF staff encourage clients to take ownership of managing their apartments. Every opportunity to make a decision increases the client's sense of ownership, self-confidence, and mastery.

Loneliness

Clients can frequently feel very lonely when living in their own apartment for the first time. Loneliness coupled with addiction disorder is a recipe for trouble. The most frequent cause for failure in the PHF program (about 10 to 15 percent) is related to excessive drug use involving a number of people. Clients who are lonely are vulnerable; they seek out others to alleviate the loneliness. Social drug use often enters the picture, and then the beer turns to crack and the client may soon be facing eviction. Staff must take a very active role in helping clients develop ways to cope with loneliness and to manage their physical and interpersonal space.

One useful way to address this problem is for PHF staff to visit frequently during the week and at different times of the day. Loneliness can also be tempered by connecting the client with natural peer support groups and the team's peer specialist. Peer specialists are often able to connect in a way that is comfortable and nonthreatening (see chapter 4 for more detail). Peer specialists can often get the client involved in a variety of activities and events both in the recovery community and in the wider surrounding community. The peer specialist can also model how to connect with others informally and show the client how to engage and develop new friendships.

Pets

Keeping a pet can be an effective tool for combatting loneliness. It can be a very rewarding experience for clients, providing them with opportunities to experience the positive self-regard that comes from caring for another. Pets can lessen stress and anxiety, provide opportunities to experience bonding, and teach responsibility.

However, with pets also come challenges. For instance, suppose a client has signed a lease that clearly indicates a no-pet policy, but, since moving in, he or she has adopted a stray cat. Of course, much depends on the size of the building and how effectively the no-pet rule is enforced, but conflict between landlords and tenants over pets is a possibility. Frequently, though, landlords are flexible and willing to give clients a chance to have a pet.

By caring for pets, clients can learn how to provide for another, think beyond themselves, budget for another's needs, and become responsible for the health needs of another: all of these are great skill-building areas.

Landlords

> *Usually you get people who are in need and they come here and they enjoy living somewhere like this instead of some of the other places they might come from. Here you get more of a residential feeling. You know it's just a sense of satisfaction, I guess, that these people get off the streets and they come here. They just need some help and they're getting it from the program.*
>
> **—Pathways Housing First landlord**

Landlords make Pathways Housing First possible. This simple fact cannot be overstated. Landlords are our essential partners. To succeed, every PHF program must establish productive and mutually rewarding business relationships with members of the real estate community, which includes landlords as well as their agents, real estate brokers, management companies, and other entities that operate affordable housing. Frequent communication among PHF teams, landlords, and clients helps ensure good housing outcomes for everybody involved.

Remember, the relationship among landlords, tenants, and the PHF program is primarily a business relationship that works to the benefit of all parties. The win-win-win relationship is created because landlords, clients, and the PHF program all have the same goal: to manage and maintain affordable, decent housing.

Benefits for PHF Landlords

There are many compelling reasons why landlords want to do business with a PHF program. Let's examine a few of those benefits.

Rent is always paid in full and on time

A model tenant always pays the rent in full and on time, and the client and PHF program must strive to be model tenants. From the program's perspective, paying rent in full and on time is a significant step toward ensuring that the landlord will rent the next vacant unit to another PHF client.

From the landlord's perspective, the most efficient process for receiving rent payments is to receive a single check from the PHF program: a check that includes both the tenant's contribution and the program's rent supplement. But sometimes payments are split: if the client is eligible for a shelter allowance or housing subsidy, the program facilitates arrangements for the government to mail this directly to the landlord. Housing and clinical staff must work proactively with clients and landlords to help them maintain the reporting and renewals that may be required. The program staff tries to reduce what the landlord is required to do, and tries to eliminate any lapses in reimbursement. This includes reminding clients of annual lease renewals, recertification appointments, and inspections.

If problems arise and a client stops paying his or her portion of the rent, then the program may have to pay that share as a loan to the client. If there are repeated instances of rent nonpayment, the program may have to either actively assist the person by making regular payments or by becoming the client's formal or informal payee, trustee, or third-party trustee. Regardless of the problem, however, the bottom line for the landlord remains the same: the rent gets paid.

PHF clients rarely have much money, and creating a workable budget can be challenging. The team must be willing to teach each client the nuts and bolts of creating a budget and sticking to it. These lessons should be repeated as often as requested or needed. As most people know, it can be difficult to keep to a budget when unplanned expenses occur or when a four-week budget lands in a month with five weeks. However, such events may be easy to foresee and quickly rectified—they should not be a reason for clients to fall behind in rent.

The apartments will not be vacant; there will be no rent loss as a result of vacancies

By working with a PHF program that is always receiving referrals, landlords are unlikely to lose revenue through apartment vacancies. If a tenant vacates a unit before the term of the lease for any reason—for example, long-term hospitalization or relocation to another unit—the PHF program makes every effort to provide another tenant as quickly as possible. When this happens, landlords are typically flexible as long as the program pays the rent in the interim or brings another tenant into the apartment and rent continues to be paid without interruption.

*The housing and clinical service teams also support the landlord,
and they come when the landlord calls*

PHF programs primarily support program clients; however, they are also a source of support to landlords. Landlords are given the 24/7 on-call cell phone number of the support services team and are encouraged to call the service team or housing staff whenever they have concerns about the well-being or behavior of a client. It is comforting for the landlord to know there is a responsible agency to call with any concerns about a tenant. On the program side, it is important to respond to every call, even if only to acknowledge that the landlord's call was received. In this way, program staff contribute to the success of the program by building a trusting and productive long-term relationship with landlords.

PHF programs are proactive in repairing damages

The PHF program repairs any damage clients cause to apartments. While this matter does not need to be communicated to the landlord, it should be part of program policy and practice, and the relatively minor expenses should be part of the budget. Repairing a hole in the wall goes a long way toward maintaining a healthy landlord relationship and toward guaranteeing that additional apartments will be available to other clients when needed.

*The landlord is helping a homeless individual leave a shelter
or the street for a permanent home*

Landlords often enjoy knowing that they are helping to end homelessness and making a significant contribution to their communities. Hosting an annual landlord appreciation dinner is a good idea.

Collaborative Roles in Housing PHF Clients

Landlords are part of any PHF transaction. Depending on the program, some of the other team members' roles may vary. Let's look at one team member who is consistently involved: the housing specialist.

The Housing Specialist

Every PHF program must have a housing specialist who works with the team, with the clients, and with landlords to address all concerns from their various perspectives.

The housing specialist should be able to do the following:

- perform initial and annual inspections of apartments

- identify potential or existing problems in apartments

- make apartment repairs or coordinate with contractors to make them

- work with local contacts and real estate brokers to identify units

The housing specialist plays a key role in the program, since PHF teams can more efficiently conduct their clinical work knowing that a designated staff member is addressing property management and maintenance issues.

Working with an Outside Housing Authority or Agency

In situations when a PHF program operates only the clinical team, the program works with an outside housing authority or housing agency to locate, rent, and furnish the apartments for clients. The housing provider works with the PHF program to locate an appropriate apartment for each client based on needs and preferences. Because PHF does not refuse individuals based on the concept of housing readiness, substance use, criminal records, and so forth, the housing provider working with the PHF program, in turn, cannot refuse these individuals for apartment placement regardless of perceived housing readiness.

Other than those placed on all tenants, no additional contingencies should be placed on the client's housing by the housing agency. The agency should work closely with the clinical team if there is an issue with the client or the apartment. The agency must also agree to re-house rapidly when required and must be committed to scattered-site, integrated, quality housing for all clients.

The Clinical Team's Role in Housing

The clinical team works closely with the housing agency to ensure that an appropriate apartment is located. The clinical team attends every meeting, accompanies the client when he or she views apartments, and, after the client selects one, works with the housing agency to expedite the lease signing.

Usually the clinical team ensures that the apartment is fully furnished and equipped, with all utilities functioning by the client's move-in day. As previously mentioned, it is helpful to have agreements with furniture providers or local furniture banks for specific furniture packages. This ensures that furnishing the apartment does not slow the move-in process. The clinical team also ensures that the rent is paid on time and works with the client to establish a monthly budget so that all utilities are paid in full on their due date. At times, PHF staff may serve as the payee or trustee of a client who is having trouble prioritizing rent and utility payments.

Although both the clinical and housing services provided to clients under the PHF model are separate, they must be highly coordinated. It is essential for the housing staff and clinical staff to meet at least weekly, because both teams are often needed to address problems as they arise. For example, the clinical team may be alerted to a broken window or a nonfunctioning stove or light switch. The clinical team or the client alerts the housing staff, who then work with the building manager and the client to set up a time for this repair. This can go very smoothly if the teams are working well together, but if not, it can become a great source of frustration and difficulty for everyone involved.

Another area requiring close communication is the tracking and reporting of outcomes to governing authorities and funding agencies. The best way to do this is by maintaining frequent, clear communication between housing and clinical services. Seamless coordination is absolutely key. Clinical and housing staff must be open with each other about their concerns and priorities, and both teams must be committed to Housing First and client-driven care.

Some Common Property Management Challenges

It is a simple fact of life that any apartment renter will have occasional maintenance issues. Since PHF clients are often renting for the very first time in their lives, they will sometimes require assistance. The best remedy, of course, is prevention. The PHF team may need to spend considerable time orienting the newly housed client to apartment life—and simultaneously gaining insight about other potential areas for assistance.

A preemptive discussion about locking and securing doors and windows, checking the stove before leaving, turning faucets off, and checking the doorbell and mailbox, can go a long way toward helping a client successfully transition into a new home. History has shown that a number of issues tend to repeat predictably, and they are discussed below. While the list is by no means exhaustive, it is offered as a precaution to help PHF teams plan and anticipate.

Keys

Once housed, clients now have in their possession two or three small items they did not have to carry before—keys. Although keys were discussed earlier, they bear further mention because keys constitute a high-frequency property management problem for both clients and staff. PHF team members must instruct clients on how to use their new keys and on the importance of keeping them in an easy-to-remember place. They help clients identify how to best carry their keys when they are out in the community, and they help them understand the importance of not making copies of keys for friends or family who do not live with them. If a client loses his or her keys and can't get into the apartment, he or she will call either the landlord or the team for assistance. Clinical teams should have copies of all tenants' keys for emergency situations.

Plumbing Issues

Water issues are not uncommon, especially in older buildings and often with older tenants. From time to time, some PHF clients have to be reminded to completely turn off running water, to completely close the shower curtain when bathing, and to make sure floors and walls stay dry during showers. Failure to close the shower curtain is a common source of water damage to the client's bathroom and, even worse, water can leak through the floor into the apartment below. When water damage occurs, landlords may demand that the client be held responsible for the damage and that he or she be charged an additional fee in rent to cover the repairs. To avoid repeated and costly repairs, the PHF program may decide in some instances to fit the apartment with automatic self-shut faucets.

Some Health and Safety Hazards

PHF staff may find it necessary to educate clients about maintaining a clean and healthy environment regarding trash disposal, laundry, expired foods, and regular apartment cleaning. The best teaching method is to demonstrate or model the task. For example, a staff member could go to the grocery store with the client, purchase the correct-size trash bags for the kitchen and bathroom, and then, together, place the bags into the bins. For disposal of trash—where and when—it can be helpful to create a calendar or other reminder system. Very concrete help is often needed in these matters. It is common for a PHF team member to meet the client for a home visit and help the client remove trash from the apartment to the designated place. If an issue persists, the team members will need to adjust their level of support until the client masters this skill. Creativity is often required.

Clutter can also be a significant challenge when it impinges on the health and safety of the client and other tenants in the building. It is best to deal with this issue right away. Being able to assist the client with these kinds of challenges depends on the relationship a PHF team member has established with the client. It may take a while to understand the meaning of the clutter. Is it a lifelong habit that perhaps was learned from his or her family? Is it related to living so long with so little that it is hard to let go of items, even if they may seem inconsequential to others? Is it a manifestation of a larger anxiety issue? The only way to know and be of assistance is to maintain a good working alliance by learning *about* the client *from* the client.

In extreme cases, if the clutter reaches unacceptable levels or constitutes a health hazard, the team may have to take action, for instance, by cleaning and removing clutter against the tenant's wishes, for the sake of the client and other tenants. Such action may ultimately prevent eviction.

Personal Relationships: Building and Reconnecting

Once housed, many clients begin to think about reconnecting with family and old friends, making new friends, or connecting to social networks, support groups, or special interest groups. Assistance with connecting with other people is a very high priority for many clients. Some clients may be eager to reconnect with family and meet new people, while others may initially rely primarily on the PHF team for their social support. For some clients, relationships develop spontaneously after they are housed and settled; for others, this may be a more difficult road.

An independent apartment can present a number of potential learning opportunities for clients with psychiatric disabilities who may have challenges connecting with others. The PHF team can support clients with their socialization goals through role-play exercises on how to greet new neighbors, providing information and support on attending community or self-help groups, and helping a client develop an online dating profile. Again, the teams tailor the support to the self-defined goals of the client.

Problematic Relationships

There are times when a client may become involved with someone who is a threat to his or her recovery or housing. This usually involves drug use and related illegal behavior, and, ultimately, the client will decide on a course of action. Regardless of those decisions—even those resulting in arrest or eviction—the responsibility of the PHF team is to be present, to offer support, and to help the client see the discrepancies between previously stated goals and what this particular relationship is doing to his or her life.

When such a relationship develops, the team needs to work closely with the client to help determine whether the client is freely choosing it or is participating under duress. If the client chooses not to be in this relationship and is looking for assistance, a team has many options. Often, showing up more frequently and at unexpected times—and showing up in pairs or more—can create an atmosphere that is uncomfortable for unwanted visitors, especially if they are engaging in illegal activities. It can also be useful to calmly explain to the unwanted visitor that he or she is not on the lease and must leave or else other action will be necessary. Threatening legal action is often useful for entrenched and unwanted guests. The team may also need to sit with the client and help him or her call the police and file a complaint. Finally, it may be necessary to work with the client to find another unit. As ever, the goal is to help clients learn from such experiences, so they can feel increasingly confident in their abilities to better maintain their apartments and their lives.

Children

A positive social challenge occurs when a client gives birth to a child or when a child previously removed from custody is returned. Both can be very rewarding experiences with countless opportunities for growth and healing. But these events can also create housing issues that need to be carefully managed. Suddenly, an apartment may be too small, or a client may need to find a neighborhood with schools, parks, and more resources for families.

PHF staff (working with both the client and the landlord) can usually coordinate such housing changes. They may also need to partner with an outside agency that is involved with the care of the client's child. This can help the PHF team to support the client in meeting any expectations that he or she is required to meet. The team also works with the client to revise the goal plan to address the client's needs in the new role of parent.

When Relocation Is Necessary

Team members practicing the PHF model understand that regardless of whether a client accepts support services with a new apartment, there is a chance that he or she might not adhere to the rules and responsibilities specified in the lease or Use and Occupancy Agreement. It is also realistic to expect that, on occasion, some clients will engage in actions that could potentially lead to long-term hospitalization, incarceration, and apartment eviction. Relapses do occur. Team members understand that relapses are part and parcel of mental illness and addiction. They are part of the journey to recovery, and they must be dealt with one event at a time.

The PHF model also maintains that, as with anyone else's life, unforeseen circumstances often necessitate a move to a new location. Therefore, moving is often considered a routine part of program operations, and arrangements are handled as rapidly and with as little added stress as possible.

Relocations and Mandatory Evictions

The ACT or ICM team decides who is admitted into the PHF program and who will get housing. Staff from the housing department or housing agency that is finding and renting apartments for the program also meet with every client—but never to determine eligibility or admission. Their role at their point of entry is to interview the client and learn about the client's housing preferences and, to some extent, any relevant housing history, so as to best accommodate the client's wishes.

After the client has moved in, and if there are problems to the extent that the client has violated the lease, the decision whether to evict or relocate the client is no longer solely under the control of the clincal team. The landlord, the housing department or agency, the team, and the client all have some influence on how these decisions are made.

Many clients who get their own apartment through the PHF program have spent years living a daily existence focused on surviving and meeting the basic needs of food and shelter. Their primary concerns have been "What am I going to eat today?" "Where will I sleep tonight?" and "Where can I use the bathroom?" If they have been struggling with substance use, their worries may have been "Where will I get my next drink? Next hit? Next cigarette?" Answering these questions on a day-to-day basis was stressful and time-consuming, and yet, at the same time, these pursuits gave purpose to their day.

Once a client moves into an apartment, many of these questions disappear. For some clients, this means a day filled with nothing to do. One new tenant had this to say on the subject: "I waited so long to get housing, then one day it happened, and I was so happy. But then I was depressed but I didn't understand why. I wasn't homeless any more. I had a nice apartment, a beautiful bed, TV, cable, dishes, towels, and food. I guess I was lonely. I wanted companionship, I wanted something to do."

It is important once clients are housed and settled into their new apartments to have conversations with them about new goals now that they have successfully met their previous goal of securing housing. Former questions about food, shelter, and safety can be replaced with questions about vocation, relationships, community, and recreation. Such conversations can often prevent potential problems and help clients dream about a new life.

In the vast majority of cases when the tenant has violated the lease, the typical scenario involves drug use and illegal inhabitants, and eviction is avoided by a quick relocation of the client into another unit. Relocations are an acceptable solution to all four parties involved. The team's relocation rate (moving clients out of their first apartment into a second) can be as high as 20 to 30 percent, especially when a high percentage of clients have severe addiction disorders. The rates of relocation from the second apartment to the third is about half the rate of the first relocation, which indicates that clients learn a lesson from losing their first unit and change their behavior to hold on to the second one.

How Mandatory Eviction Affects Client Choice

Client choice is a central guiding principle of the PHF program, but it is also one of the concepts most frequently misunderstood by those seeking to replicate the program—and even by PHF staffers and clients themselves. In the housing world, *choice* does not mean *absolute choice.* Choice of the first apartment is tempered by the economic realities of the rental market and by the state or federal "fair market value" rent stipend. There is no choice about signing a lease or paying the rent, and there is no choice regarding lease violations. The client faces the same responsibilities and consequences that other renters do. The main difference is that most other tenants in scattered-site housing do not have a case manager looking after their interests.

If a client violates the lease, the team will advocate for a second apartment—but the housing department is urged to house people who are homeless and awaiting apartments first. The request to find an apartment for a relocating client usually drops to second place in the housing priority queue, so there is less choice about how quickly the second apartment is found. If furniture is required for the second apartment, it is not provided free. There is no choice about repaying for furniture that has been sold during a relapse. The client must pay for it on an affordable monthly budget. Depending on the nature of the lease violation, choice of units may be further restricted because the client has demonstrated disruptive or threatening behavior, and this may restrict the types of buildings that the housing agency is willing to show to that client. When the client demonstrates disruptive behaviors, the program manages risk by restricting choice, but still keeps the door open and continues to work with the client through the crises until another unit is found.

Every client gets a second chance and a third chance, and then everyone begins to have doubts about the possibility of housing the client successfully. The client may have to demonstrate to the housing agency or to the team that he or she is sincere about changing habits or disruptive behavior. Some clients may have to go to detox before a fourth apartment is offered. Each failure slightly diminishes client choice. The first apartment failure is often expected; the second is even understandable, but by the third, there is no longer the assumption that the team will proceed with looking for another unit under the same contract. At this point, the client must actively persuade the housing agency and the team that this time it will be different— and describe how it will be different. This is not simply a verbal commitment. The "walk must match the talk."

While many clients who use substances are, in fact, successful in maintaining tenancy once housed, the most frequent reason for failure in the PHF program (now about 10 to 15 percent) is excessive alcohol or other drug use that involves a number of people. The "why" of this problem is complicated, and different elements come into play for each situation.

Clients who have lost apartments because of substance-related behaviors and were asked "What led to others taking over your apartment, and ultimately to the loss of your apartment?" have reported some of the following responses:

- guilt about having a place when friends from the street don't

- loneliness

- wanting to help others by letting them sleep over, shower, and eat

- using the apartment to get substances ("You bring the alcohol and other drugs; I've got the place.")

- being unable to say "no"

- not truly understanding the responsibilities of tenancy

When substance use becomes a client's primary goal and takes a higher priority than maintaining the responsibilities of tenancy, a series of events usually unfold that includes neighbor complaints, landlord complaints, and police involvement. The neglected responsibilities of tenancy that generally put an apartment lease at risk and can lead to eviction or arrest include these patterns:

- failure to pay rent

- allowing people not on the lease to live in the apartment over an extended period of time

- not keeping the place clean

- not being at home at the agreed-upon time for the visit

- inflicting damage to the premises

- using the premises for illegal purposes

- causing or permitting a nuisance or interfering with the reasonable peace, comfort, or privacy of neighbors

Focusing on a client's substance use in these situations is generally not helpful, because the client is often in denial or afraid. Focusing instead on the client's stated goal, "securing and maintaining housing," and providing information about the responsibilities in the tenant's lease, giving landlord and tenant feedback as it occurs, being supportive and nonjudgmental, and helping clients problem-solve for themselves about a course of action to take is the best use of staff time and is the best hope for clients to modify problematic behaviors that are interfering with their tenancy.

Connecting a tenant to a peer who has "been there"—someone who has lost an apartment due to substance-related behaviors—can help. Personal experience is often the most effective means of education, particularly when behavior modification is involved.

Staff work to maintain a nonjudgmental and supportive relationship with a client who is in the throes of losing an apartment due to substance-related behaviors. It is not helpful to point out perceived "failures" or "mess-ups" or to advocate for a course of action, such as sobriety. The staff job is to ask "What is your goal?" "How do you think you can achieve it?" and "How can we help?" And then to ask "How are you doing with your goal?" And again, "How can we help?"

If a client does not reach his or her goal on the first try, PHF staff's job is to help the client reflect on the experience and offer support in trying again, asking, "What was your goal?" "How did you do?" and "What do you think you will do differently next time?"

Still, there are a few clients who cannot manage the freedom of living independently. This is discovered after several apartments are "lost" and after several unsuccessful relocations. For these clients, a different type of housing arrangement is needed. A building with a secured front door will often do the trick because the client cannot control the front door and will need someone to manage that for him or her. The teams can continue to work with clients in these settings and assist them in finding other programs, or they can continue to treat and support them while they are living in another type of housing.

Housing Loss, Relocation, and Staff Attitudes

The previous passages describe the more difficult aspects of operating a PHF program. The most important thing to remember during a relapse or the chaos of relocation is to show *compassion*. In some ways, it is understandable that the housing agency, the landlord, and the team are frustrated and disappointed when a client relapses and damages a brand-new apartment. But any expression of exasperation is misplaced, and it only occurs because the providers have lost sight of who is really suffering in this situation. Who has suffered the worst and most painful consequences of this relapse? Is it the providers because they have been inconvenienced, or is it the client who suffers from self-hatred, guilt, and humiliation? The client usually feels awful about squandering a new opportunity and facing homelessness again. There are already plenty of consequences ahead, as we've described. There is no need for providers to be judgmental or express their disappointment or frustration to this client with a look or a phrase. This would be a failure of empathy and compassion. The correct clinical response to the client who has relapsed is "I am really sorry you are going through this. How can I help?"

Chapter 3 Summary

Integrated housing and scattered-site housing: Clients live in private market housing where access is not determined by disability. In any one building, no more than 20 percent of units are leased by the program.

Privacy: Clients live in their own apartments, which are equipped with private bathrooms and kitchens, and there is no expectation that clients will need to share any living areas with other tenants.

Affordable housing: Clients are not required to pay more that 30 percent of their income for housing costs.

Permanent housing tenure: There are no expected time limits on housing tenure, although the lease agreement may need to be renewed periodically.

Housing subsidy availability: The PHF program has ready access to housing subsidies or is able to provide a housing subsidy to ensure rapid and affordable housing.

Program/agency: The terms *program* and *agency* are used interchangeably to define the PHF program or an agency that is operating a Housing First program.

Rapid re-housing: The PHF program offers clients who have lost their housing the provision of new housing without preconditions. New housing units are provided quickly to avoid a gap in housing.

Use and Occupancy Agreement: This is a written agreement (similar to a sublease) between the client and PHF that specifies the rights and responsibilities of typical tenants in the community and contains agreements about the client paying 30 percent of his or her income for rent and agreeing to apartment visits from PHF staff.

Contact with clients and housing support: The team meets with the client at least once a week. The team offers ongoing support with neighborhood orientation, landlord relations, budgeting, shopping, making rental and bill payments, and connecting with community supports.

Outside housing agency: When PHF contracts with a local housing agency to provide suitable units for the program, PHF policies regarding "housing readiness" must prevail. Close cooperation among the clinical and housing service staff members is especially crucial in these circumstances.

An Interdisciplinary Approach

How the ACT and ICM Teams Serve Clients in a PHF Program

The idea, the principle, is that we're all working together toward the same goal: the person is in charge.

—Juliana Walker, training director, Pathways to Housing, Inc.

IN THE PATHWAYS HOUSING FIRST MODEL, two types of teams typically provide treatment and support services. A PHF assertive community treatment (ACT) team generally serves clients with severe psychiatric disabilities, and a PHF intensive case management (ICM) team generally serves those with more moderate disabilities. Any of these clients may also have alcohol and other substance use problems. Both of these PHF teams are community-based and interdisciplinary, and both meet clients in their own environments to flexibly provide a wide array of support and treatment services. While larger PHF programs may utilize both ACT and ICM teams, smaller programs might choose one or the other.

A Community-Based Interdisciplinary Approach

By using ACT or ICM teams, the same staff can conduct outreach and engage clients living on the streets, assist them in finding and moving into apartments, and then continue to provide treatment and support until the client graduates from the program. This kind of continuity of care is very well suited for clients with long histories of frequent and fragmented interactions with social, mental health, addiction, and criminal justice systems. It is also an effective alternative to most continuum of care systems that use separate programs to provide this array of services.

Once the client is housed and begins to feel safe and secure, the work of these support and treatment teams begins to focus on resolving other problems. The teams are prepared to assist clients with their emerging needs; these can range from legal issues to loading a washing machine, from obtaining a physical exam to seeing a psychiatrist. These are highly individualized services that move at the client's pace, because it is the client who determines the type, sequence, and intensity of the services.

The ACT or ICM team is the client's point of entry into the PHF program, and it also provides the continuity. Team members bear the responsibility of successfully engaging clients, welcoming them to the program, and demonstrating the respect and compassion that is at the foundation of all services offered by this intervention. One of the keys to the program's success is selecting and training staff members who share the humanitarian and social justice values upon which the PHF program is based.

This chapter outlines the history, philosophy, and key activities of the PHF ACT and ICM teams, including the comprehensive assessment and treatment planning process and the all-important home visit. Chapter 5 covers some of the clinical operations of the ACT team, and chapter 6 discusses ICM teams in more detail.

Matching Clients with the Right Level of Service

As noted, PHF programs can use either ACT or ICM teams to provide the treatment and support component of the program. Assertive community treatment (ACT) services are geared toward clients with more severe mental health problems. Despite the name, intensive case management services are a step *down* in intensity from ACT services. From a diagnostic perspective, ICM clients generally do not have an Axis I diagnosis of moderately severe mental illness, which includes a range of personality disorders, PTSD, behavioral characteristics, and addiction disorders that compromise their ability to manage their lives. They are also chronically homeless and frequently go in and out of detox, emergency rooms, hospitals, or jails.

A quadrant classification system can be used to describe the mix of co-occurring diagnoses.

Psychiatric Disability	High	Psychiatric Disability	High
Substance Abuse	Low	Substance Abuse	High
Psychiatric Disability	Low	Psychiatric Disability	Low
Substance Abuse	Low	Substance Abuse	High

Clients served by ACT teams would be described by the top row: all have high severity of psychiatric disability (schizophrenia, psychotic spectrum, or major depression) and can have either high or low levels of addiction. The most vulnerable group is classified as high on both psychiatric disability (PD) and substance abuse (SA) because they often also have a host of acute and chronic health problems.

Clients served by ICM would have a moderate mental illness but are still incapacitated by it; they would be rated moderate on PD (or they once had high PD but are in remission), and they can have either low or high levels of SA.

ICM services are also made available to clients on the ACT team who are recovering and who no longer need the ACT level of intensity. Because clients' lives and their diagnoses are fluid and not static or fixed entities, it is possible that the same client may start out receiving ICM services and after a time, because of their changing needs, he or she can be moved to ACT and vice versa.

Some PHF programs use ICM services to serve clients with both severe and moderate psychiatric disabilities and addiction disorders. Clients with severe mental illness are best served by an ACT team; however, an ICM team can easily be modified to be "ACT lite" by adding a part-time psychiatrist or psychiatric nurse practitioner. This is a viable option and may be necessary because of a program's funding constraints. Other agencies may need to use ICM teams because they are small programs serving fewer than thirty or forty clients and the size of the program does not support ACT staffing levels.

ACT and ICM Teams: Differences and Similarities

Let's briefly compare the two models to see how each contributes to the overall PHF program. There are a number of structural and practice differences between the ACT and ICM teams: different staffing patterns, client-to-staff ratios, and costs. Within the PHF program, ACT members tend to work as a team with clients; these teams are staffed with specialists that provide services directly. Because of the population it serves, the ACT team includes a nurse, addiction specialist, peer specialist, psychiatrist, social worker, and housing specialist. In contrast, ICM teams in the PHF program are staffed with generalists who broker specialty services. These teams work one on one with clients.

In the PHF context, the similarities of the two models exceed their differences, partly because both are usually modified to better meet the needs of the clients. Both provide around-the-clock on-call services. Both address housing issues: because they operate in a PHF context, significant time is devoted to addressing the housing needs of clients by providing the support necessary to promote the successful transformation from a lifestyle based on street survival to the citizenship required for successful community integration.

Finally, both PHF teams share the same recovery-focused treatment philosophy. Because of the continuity of treatment in this model, team members get to work closely with the clients and really get to know them. This allows a highly individualized treatment approach, which is at the foundation of a recovery-focused practice. In such an approach, there is an understanding and appreciation that no two clients are the same and that every client's journey in recovery is unique.

In the PHF context, both ACT and ICM teams provide the type of support that promotes community integration. Both connect clients with self-help and peer support groups as well as with more general supports that reinforce the recovery process, including spiritual, family, and community services. The teams also assist recovery by continuously providing choice, hope, and acceptance, and by helping clients develop meaningful, productive lives.

Comprehensive Assessment and Treatment Planning

In the PHF model, both types of teams—ACT and ICM—structure their operations around a comprehensive assessment and treatment plan for each client. This plan includes a number of life domains such as health, housing, employment, family and social network, and addiction. It also includes the client's Wellness Recovery Action Plan (WRAP, a very useful instrument developed by Mary Ellen Copeland), which reflects the client's strengths, needs, interests, and goals.

The WRAP is developed jointly with the client and defines a course of action for achieving immediate, near, and future goals. The plan provides an agenda and a structure that guide most interactions between the team and the client, the work of the team, and some of the life domains of the client. The plans are prepared carefully and with the full understanding that they reflect only a partial reality of the clients' lives, that clients have much more complex lives than what is written on their treatment plans.

While team members can help clients identify some areas in which they want to effect change in their lives, the client ultimately determines what, when, and how he or she wants to change. When a goal is identified, it is broken down into a number of action steps with a timeline for completion that the client determines. This timeline provides the client and the team with a useful map—an agenda that describes a course of action to realize each goal.

The following structure offers a framework for identifying and organizing clients' goals:

1. Client's goal

2. Client's role or steps to be taken

3. Team's role

4. Time frame or frequency of action

For example, a client might express the goal "I don't want to be stressed out." To achieve this goal, the client explains that exercise and meditation might be helpful. The client's role will be to

- exercise at the YMCA twice a week

- practice meditative breathing techniques for five minutes three times a week

The immediate next steps for the team's role will be to

- provide the client with a letter to buy a discounted YMCA membership

- plan a time to take the client on a tour of the YMCA to learn about using the facility

- have the wellness specialist review meditative breathing exercises with the client that week

During the initial assessment and treatment-planning interview that typically occur while the client is still homeless, almost invariably clients relate that housing and housing-related concerns are of primary importance. Since the PHF model provides housing without requiring the client to begin treatment, this first goal can be quickly met. Concerns such as small repairs, issues with the building management, neighbors, lease signing, rent payments, or other matters related to renting and maintaining an apartment are always a part of the housing-related goals conversation between the PHF team and the client.

With their housing goals achieved, it becomes possible for clients to begin to focus on other goals, most of which are broader and cover various aspects of the client's life. For example, clients have often lost contact with family members, but since they are now a part of the PHF program, they are in a position to renew past relationships with relatives. Clients' goals are as numerous and diverse as the clients themselves. Goals may include getting new dentures, obtaining a driver's license, visiting relatives, losing weight, eating healthy food, getting a job, getting off medication, getting on medication, reducing drug use, writing poetry, staying out of the hospital, getting a girlfriend or boyfriend, taking a photography or yoga class, going to the library, getting new eyeglasses, or becoming clean and sober.

One of the PHF program outcomes that providers of "treatment, sobriety, then housing" programs may find surprising is that most PHF clients list mental health treatment and substance abuse treatment as important goals *after* they are housed. *Moving into an apartment of their own creates a fundamental change in clients' motivation; it increases their investment in participating in the program and becoming an active participant in their own recovery.*

"Wow, I have my own place," reflected Stan, soon after moving in. "Now," he continued, "how do I keep it?" For Stan, "keeping it" meant taking immediate steps to reduce his drinking. For others, such as clients who still find it difficult to relax their vigilance or get a good night's sleep even after being housed, the next step might be seeing the program's psychiatrist to get medication that has helped them in the past. Other frequently reported goals include finding a job and a relationship. Addressing health concerns is also near the top of clients' lists.

Perhaps the most valuable lesson learned from the PHF program is that clients who are seemingly incapacitated and who face multiple challenges are, in fact, capable of setting and meeting their own goals for housing and treatment *if* they are provided with the right resources and support.

Treatment planning should be an active and dynamic process. As one goal is reached, another new goal emerges—often one never before considered possible. For example, Stan's initial goal was to stop drinking in order to keep his apartment. At that point he could not imagine that two years after his first AA meeting he would be invited to be a keynote speaker for his state's annual AA meeting. The successful realization of one goal creates opportunities to develop and achieve higher ones— goals that may have once been unimaginable.

The journey of recovery is an individual journey, and it is a journey of awakenings. Each client must be awakened from their hopelessness and helped to realize his or her own dreams. Many clients have had their hopes and dreams dashed by years of homelessness and negative, stigmatizing myths about mental illness and addiction. Team members can play a very useful role in the awakening and goal-setting process. Ideally, this is a synergistic process in which team members develop a trusting and collaborative relationship with clients, asking the important questions that invite and challenge clients to consider constructing a life that was once beyond their dreams.

The Art and Science of the Home Visit

The home visit is the heart and soul of the work we do, because I think that's ultimately where you want the change to happen, you know, in the person's environment.

—Adam Fussaro, Pathways to Housing Philadephia

Conducting a home visit is one the most important interventions for the clinical and support services teams. The client's home is the stage where many of the team services are performed. In this section we will define the elements of the home visit and describe how to conduct an effective one.

The home visit serves many purposes. It is both casual and focused. On any given day, PHF team members must make many home visits, so they need to be efficient, prepared, and organized. This is not simply a social call; it is a targeted intervention. In the words of Buddy Garfinkle, MSW, a training consultant for Pathways to Housing New York:

> If you start to run the numbers and you see how much time you have for face-to-face contact with individuals—it's not that much. It's really not that much. How many people on your team's caseload? Sixty? Eighty? A hundred? You make the home visit, you better have a good idea of what it is that you're trying to accomplish.

The home visit is not like a formal therapy session, but since it is a clinician who is visiting the home of a client, there is treatment going on. The team member is not visiting to provide a prescribed treatment—the home visit is more like a visit to invite the client to participate in treatment or develop a plan for productive, meaningful activity.

The emotional tone is much like that of a visit with a relative. It begins with a warm, respectful greeting: "Good to see you." "How are you?" The conversation begins with the issues currently being addressed by the client and the team, usually the ones discussed during the treatment or WRAP plan session, and it may evolve into developing new plans or activities. The visit is warm, caring, and casual—but it is also a mandatory, targeted intervention. Balancing all of those different and somewhat orthogonal components requires a thoughtful and insightful approach, which is why we refer to the *art and science* of the home visit.

For best results in ensuring the client is home when the team visits, the visit must be scheduled in advance. It is useful to schedule all home visits for the month at the beginning of each month and at a time that is convenient for the client. In this way, the client can anticipate and prepare for the visit. Team members prepare for the home visit by reading the client's most recent progress notes and reviewing the client's goals, so there can be effective follow-up during the visit.

Often, a visit starts in the home and ends up in the community. (For an example, see ICM team leader Sarah Knight's daily log in chapter 6.) Team members often meet clients at their homes and escort them to a clinic or other appointment, or meet them at home and then go shopping with them or take a walk around the neighborhood. These outings are important because they also provide the team member an opportunity to observe how clients interact with others in their own communities.

The primary purpose of the home visit is to ensure the client's well-being. The home visit provides a candid picture of how a client is managing in the apartment and in the building. The team can also observe the client's mood, health status, and physical condition. Above all, the purpose of a home visit is to check in and monitor a client's progress from week to week.

The second most important reason for the home visit is to ensure that clients are managing well as tenants and that their apartments are in good shape. In partnership with the client, the PHF program is also responsible for the apartment, especially in instances when the program is paying a significant portion of the rent. In some sense, the program is like a housing provider, and it assumes the risks of a housing provider. For example, if anything breaks in the apartment—not because of what the client does, but from natural wear and tear—the team member can help the client assess the damage during the next home visit and contact the landlord. If the client asks for help, the team member can call the landlord and advocate on the client's behalf.

Much can be observed during a home visit, notes Ben Henwood of Pathways to Housing Philadelphia:

> When you're doing home visits, you'll just get a lot of information. I mean some people are still in their place after a months and what you see is the furniture they moved in with, and groceries that they've bought, and there's nothing else in there. . . some people will live like that for a while. There are others who will move in right away and make it more of a home by putting pictures up and having personal effects around.

Team members can learn an enormous amount about clients by carefully observing their living spaces. They might notice half-empty wine bottles on the kitchen counter. They might wonder, who are the people in the new picture taped to the fridge? Whose shoes are those placed next to the client's by the doorway? How comfortable is the client in his or her home? Has he or she unpacked everything since moving in? What is the condition of the apartment: tidy or messy? Is there evidence that the client cooks meals? These observations and questions may be addressed or they may also be stored as points of reference and can be returned to during a future visit. This is a long-term relationship, and engagement, trust, and disclosure travel on a long-term trajectory.

Answers to these questions and observing the client's mood and response to the visit will inform the way the team approaches the client, which could prevent a possible psychiatric or housing crisis. Adam Fussaro, MSW, of Pathways to Housing Philadelphia, put it this way:

> You get certain cues—like if the person is typically talkative and they're kind of reserved. That might be a cue that something is going on. If they're usually well groomed and if they have a less clean look, then maybe things are kind of deteriorating psychiatrically. You get clues into what's really going on in their apartment. And, on the practical side, you can support people better that way.

Another purpose of the home visit is to provide services such as counseling, medication delivery, and practical support, such as bringing medication or tools to help a client fix a leaky faucet. Treatment visits, however, can be daunting for some clients and require patience and creativity. For example, one of the team nurses needed to make daily visits to a client with severe diabetes in order to check her blood sugar level. The client was very frightened of the needle stick and initially resisted the test. To help make the visit and the procedure as comfortable as possible, the client and nurse informally developed a routine wherein the nurse enters the apartment and says hello, and the client says hello and sits down. The nurse then gets a glass of water for the client and they spend the next several minutes talking about the client's favorite sports team. Eventually, the nurse asks to check the client's blood sugar level, and the client agrees.

Yet another purpose of the home visit is to create an opportunity to connect and work on developing a deeper and more authentic relationship with the client. To do this, team members must be focused, but not hurried. Building a relationship takes time—especially when some clients are suspicious of a team's motives and are convinced that the team has the power to take the apartment away (which they do not). During the early phases of the program, clients may deny problems or troubling issues they face. To foster trust, team members must convey acceptance and concern—not judgment.

Consider the following exchange between Jen Walker and Ben Henwood, staffers at Pathways to Housing Philadelphia.

Ben: You know this is a long process and it's really getting to know people…

Jen: We're in the very baby stages of these relationships that are going to be very long term, which is exciting, but progress can be slow in terms of getting to know folks and having a level of trust that enables them to tell us what's really going on. I also still feel like with most of my clients, it's like, "When is the other shoe going to drop? When are they going to catch me doing something that's going to mean I'm going to lose my apartment?" They still want to put on this front that everything's fine.

Ben: And we've seen that play out. There was a couple that was living together and both were using and hiding their IV drug use from us. We slowly talked about that, and we talked about needle exchange and harm reduction. A week later, we got a call from one of them saying, "My partner's overdosed. I didn't know who to call and I called you." And that was the opportunity for us to go over. It was a life-and-death situation and that changed things. Since then, the conversation has looked a lot different. I think that's when they finally realized they could talk to us about what's going on. Up until then they felt like they needed to hide it. So, it takes time and it takes those sorts of occasions sometimes. There was nothing we could have done up until then that would have convinced them otherwise.

One of the interesting things about a home visit is the way it creates a shift in power dynamics between client and staff. The home visit, after all, occurs on the client's own turf. This, coupled with the PHF program philosophy that housing is a right and not dependent on a client's participation in treatment, poses an interesting challenge for the team member. The challenge for the staff is to engage the client into treatment when treatment is not mandatory. Short, hurried visits or an absent client when the team comes to call can be indications that the team is *not* engaging well with a client. The client's degree of engagement can be one indicator of the staff's clinical skills. Another measure of the team's success is the extent to which they are warmly welcomed into their clients' apartments.

Surprise home visits should occur only if there are concerns that a client is in danger or hurt and only after all other ways to contact the client have been exhausted. It is rarely necessary for PHF team members to use their duplicate keys to enter a client's home after several warnings, but it does occasionally happen. Buddy Garfinkle, training consultant at Pathways to Housing New York, had this comment:

> There are no stinkin' rules in ACT or ICM. You better provide services to people that are in line with what they want or they're not going to open the door, or they're going to be in the house and they're going to pretend they're not there, or they're not going to be there when they know that you're coming, or when you walk in they're going to flip you off—because they can. So, the whole power dynamic changes in ACT, and that's a good thing.

The home visit, both in its form and content, provides a wealth of information about the client, the client's living conditions, the staff, and the condition of the treatment relationship. It is a microcosm of the entire program. Most of the work of the program takes place during the home visit. The teams continue to visit their clients and they bring them caring and questions: "How are you?" "How can I help you?" They try to keep the door open, and they seek to open new doors, all by asking the right questions.

Renewing Team Practice and Team Process

In the Pathways Housing First program setting, it is very useful for clinical teams to devote one meeting per month (or more during start-up) to exploring their own team process. Day-to-day life on either an ACT or an ICM team is very busy and allows little time for personal reflection, let alone reflecting on team process. The team can review its efficiencies and inefficiencies, examine incidents that were managed well and others in which there is clear room for improvement, develop team goals much like the team does for clients, and even create a Wellness Recovery Action Plan for the team.

On occasion, the PHF team is well served by a day-long team retreat. A retreat is a great time to reflect on one's own work and the work of the team, to relax and enjoy each other's company, and to replenish and recharge for the work ahead.

Chapter 4 Summary

In the Pathways to Housing program, clinical and support services are provided by **assertive community treatment (ACT) teams** and/or **intensive case management (ICM) teams**. ACT teams generally serve clients with severe psychiatric disorders and work as a team; ICM teams serve those with moderate psychiatric disorders. While an ACT team is typically composed of specialists, ICM teams are composed of generalists who work individually; they also broker services from other agencies and entities. Both types of teams manage a wide array of clinical and support services, delivered mostly in the client's own environment.

For both ACT and ICM teams, the clinical relationship to the client is based on a **comprehensive assessment and treatment plan**. This plan covers a number of life domains such as health, housing, employment, family and social network, and addiction. It also includes the client's Wellness Recovery Action Plan (WRAP), which is based on the client's strengths, needs, interests, and goals.

Both types of teams also conduct **home visits** with clients. These visits occur frequently when a new client occupies an apartment, then typically taper to once a week, then less often over time. The home visit offers the clinical team insight into the client's health, well-being, and adjustment to the apartment and the community. It also offers an opening for discussing goals and other treatment-related topics.

The PHF Assertive Community Treatment Team

THIS CHAPTER DESCRIBES THE ASSERTIVE community treatment (ACT) model and describes some of the ACT team's clinical operations in the context of Pathways Housing First: how the team functions, how it is staffed, and how it runs the daily morning meeting that keeps all its members informed.

In this daily ritual, all ACT team members meet and review each client's status, review work completed to date, and plan the tasks for the day or days ahead. In the context of the morning meeting, this chapter also outlines the "boards and logs" method of scheduling staff time and tracking client and team data. This system has many useful features, and, although computerized systems have been developed, we include the boards and logs system in this manual to illustrate the many details a team needs to consider during the morning meeting in order to deliver optimal services for its clients. A hypothetical morning meeting is described, and the chapter concludes with a brief discussion of the weekly conference review.

Assertive Community Treatment Teams:
How They Work in a PHF Program

When we moved our services out of the hospital and started working with people in their own community, we discovered that people were capable of so much more than we had imagined possible.

—Leonard I. Stein, M.D., cofounder of the assertive community treatment model

Assertive community treatment (ACT) is one of the most widely embraced and well-documented community mental health programs for treating those with severe mental illness. In the ACT model, a multidisciplinary team delivers a full range of medical, psychosocial, and rehabilitative services to clients in a *community*—rather than institutional—setting. When a PHF program seeks to serve homeless clients with severe psychiatric disabilities who often have health and addiction problems, an ACT team is a highly effective treatment and support approach for achieving the best results.

To fully appreciate how PHF uses these teams, it is useful to take a look at ACT's origins. What we now know as the assertive community treatment model began in the 1970s as the Training in Community Living program in Madison, Wisconsin. Here, a dedicated and insightful group of clinicians working in an inpatient psychiatric unit realized something: if they wanted clients who were repeatedly admitted and discharged from the hospital to successfully remain in the community, they would have to develop an effective way to provide treatment and support *in* that community. They then created a community-based team modeled after the staffing pattern of the inpatient unit. This "hospital without walls" consisted of people from multiple disciplines who worked together, met daily, and coordinated care for a specified group of clients. Such was the beginning of ACT.

Since its founding by Leonard I. Stein, M.D., Mary Ann Test, Ph.D. and Arnold Marx, M.D., this model has shown itself to be a remarkably robust and flexible way to treat people with severe mental illness. Today, ACT is a clearly defined intervention with a widely used fidelity scale [16] that measures the quality of its implementation in the areas of human resources, organizational boundaries, and nature of services. It has proven itself very useful in serving a population that has multiple needs and had been using multiple service providers to address them. The ACT team's interdisciplinary staff can provide much of the care directly, making it much easier for clients to obtain high-quality care coupled with excellent continuity.

In practice, ACT teams assume full professional responsibility for addressing clinical needs and for providing concrete assistance in the skills of daily living—from help with managing symptoms to budgeting and paying the rent. ACT services are intensive, with daily visits for some clients. These visits usually take place in clients' homes or in the community. By taking a bold step out of the comfort of their institutional setting and into their clients' communities, the innovators of ACT helped increase clients' community tenure and their possibilities for recovery.

The ACT model has now been studied for more than thirty years, and several researchers have identified its critical components and compared them to similar approaches. These are some of ACT's key features:

- interdisciplinary staffing that includes expertise in psychiatry, nursing, social work, vocational functioning, substance abuse treatment, and related fields

- a team approach (shared caseloads and daily team meetings)

- low staff-client ratios (1:10)

- locus of contact in the community

- intensive and frequent contacts with clients

- assertive outreach

- ready access in times of crisis (twenty-four-hour availability)

- time-unlimited services

Recently, the U.S. Health and Human Services' Substance Abuse and Mental Health Services Administration (SAMHSA) endorsed ACT as an evidence-based practice, which led to a surge of interest in the model. Today, assertive community treatment has been implemented throughout the world.

Although specific admission criteria may vary across service systems or programs, ACT services are usually reserved for clients with a so-called Axis I disorder of severe mental illness (schizophrenia or schizoaffective disorder, bipolar disorder, or major depression). Within the Pathways Housing First program, ACT teams serve vulnerable clients with severe mental illness, and most also have co-occurring substance abuse diagnoses, multiple health problems that often result in frequent hospital or emergency room use, arrests or incarceration, and long histories of homelessness. To address these needs for PHF, the ACT team's staff includes an integrated dual disorders specialist, a primary care professional, and a housing specialist.

Notably, ACT teams that do not function within the PHF model and do not have direct access to housing are *not* as effective in providing continuity of care to this segment of the homeless population. If a team is serving homeless clients and does not have access to housing, most of that team's time will be spent searching for a place for their clients to live. PHF, on the other hand, immediately secures housing for clients and provides a base of operation so the team can proceed with providing clinical services. Clients find it easier to engage in services with the ACT team within the Pathways context, and clients begin to use fewer acute care services by receiving services in their homes, where they feel more comfortable and secure.

As ACT teams evolved, they began to include a variety of highly trained clinicians. This interdisciplinary model means that, although there are indeed specialists on the team, the scope and goals of the team's work with each individual client are joint responsibilities. Team members share skills and information with each other, and clients are actively engaged in determining their own comprehensive plans for recovery. Teams consist of specialists in substance abuse, supported employment, family systems treatment, and wellness management recovery (also known as illness management recovery). Teams also include peer specialists—current or former recipients of mental health services—and may include other specialists, such as an occupational therapist or housing specialist, depending upon the clients' needs. In the PHF program, each team also has a part-time psychiatrist and a part-time physician or nurse practitioner to address medical needs.

Within PHF, the ACT team offers services that are grounded in the principles of recovery. This marks a conscious and deliberate shift away from the medical "clinician as expert" approach inherent in the original "hospital without walls" model. And it marks a move towards embracing a recovery orientation in which the client is directly involved as an active participant and decision maker in all aspects of the treatment plan. The client chooses what type of service is needed, its pace, and its intensity. While ACT teams can provide many PHF services directly, most of these services are in the treatment range, and the team should be fully prepared to help the client locate or engage in services in the community, for example, self-help groups or reconnecting with family or other supports. The frequency of contact varies depending on the client's condition and needs. A client who is not doing well may be visited once or twice a day, whereas someone doing well might be seen weekly. Clients generally set the pace for the contact.

While client choice determines the vast majority of treatment, and the PHF support services provided by ACT may seem limitless, there are, in fact, quite definite limits to client choice. In crisis situations, such as when a client is having a psychotic episode and has become afraid of the team, the team must be very assertive and see the client very frequently—even if the client resists these visits—in order to try to avoid a hospitalization. However, it is possible that, despite the team's best efforts, a client may need to be involuntarily hospitalized. There are clear definitions in the mental hygiene law of what constitutes a danger to self or others. These must be explained clearly and carefully to the client, and they must be followed.

The team continues to work with the client through the hospitalization (assisting in the hospitalization), and then works with the inpatient team to plan the discharge process. The continuity of relationship through the crisis is a key component of building a stronger and more trusting relationship with the client. After the psychotic symptoms abate, the client often acknowledges that he or she understands that the intention of the team is to help. Even in a crisis, the team's caring is noted and appreciated. At times, a team will have to wait a while to regain a client's trust.

When working with clients who are at high risk for hospitalization, it is recommended that the team develop a Wellness Recovery Action Plan (WRAP), advanced directives, or other relapse prevention plans with the client. These plans will provide a means for the team to take clients' wishes into account during times when they may not be able to express them. In this way, clients are active participants, choosing who should be included in their support network and involved in their crisis plan.

The ACT Team Members

> *It's a high-energy job; I mean, it does take a lot of work. But the rewards are so great. The relationships are everything— the relationships that we have with each other, and the relationships that we have with the people we serve.*

> **—Juliana Walker, training director, Pathways to Housing, Inc.**

As mentioned before, the PHF assertive community treatment (ACT) team is interdisciplinary, with all members sharing a vision grounded in the Pathways model and in recovery principles. Each team is composed of some mix of the members listed below. Staffing is based on a 1:10 caseload ratio, so a seven-member team serves seventy clients. The primary care specialist, housing specialist, and administrative assistant do not count as part of the staffing pattern because in many agencies these positions are provided by another agency.

PHF ACT teams may include these members:

- team leader

- psychiatrist (part time, 1:100 ratio)

- primary care practitioner (part time, 1:200 ratio; could be a family practice doctor or a nurse practitioner)

- nurse

- peer specialist (a current or former recipient of mental health services)

- family systems specialist (optional)

- occupational therapist (optional)

- mental health specialist (often a social worker)

- wellness management specialist (also known as an illness management recovery specialist)

- employment specialist (using the Individual Placement and Support or Supported Employment model)

- substance abuse specialist (trained in integrated dual disorders treatment, or IDDT)

- program assistant

All specialists also serve as service coordinators responsible for general case management activities. All team members have a "we will do whatever it takes" attitude toward helping clients, viewing their job descriptions flexibly.

The Team Leader

Imagine the PHF assertive community treatment team as a bicycle wheel. Team members are the spokes that support the rim, each spoke working equally to provide the structure, wholeness, and strength that allows the entire wheel to move forward. Every wheel must have a hub. The hub provides the anchor or support for each of the spokes and reinforces their contact with the perimeter, or outside world.

In this analogy, the team leader is the hub. He or she organizes, motivates, coaches, trains, and supports the team by providing organizational structure, clinical team supervision, one-on-one mentorship of team members, in-the-field leadership, and philosophical direction. The team leader also serves as the liaison with the agency's administration.

Since one responsibility of the leader is to train ACT team members and be a positive role model, excellent clinical skills are key. Organizational skills are also needed to manage a treatment team that serves adults with severe co-occurring diagnoses who are living independently in the community in apartments rented from local landlords. The team leader must manage the sometimes competing priorities and demands of all of these stakeholders to operate a successful program.

As clinical supervisor, the team leader seeks to help ACT team members enhance their skills, particularly in handling difficult situations and issues. The team leader also helps in other clinical areas, including formulating collaborative, comprehensive treatment plans, addressing problematic situations with clients or other team members, and managing time while ensuring that clients receive all necessary services.

As a clinical supervisor, the team leader should be very familiar with the regulatory demands of the program's city, state, and federal funding sources and assure that team practice is consistent with these standards. The team leader also needs to understand the services and financial supports related to health, mental health, addictions, income support, and housing stipends within the clients' communities. A team leader with this knowledge is better able to support the team as it carries out its day-to-day duties of providing optimal services to program clients.

As a mentor, the team leader provides one-on-one supervision by meeting with each team member once a week. In these meetings, team members are encouraged to discuss specific cases or situations with which they need assistance, and the team leader offers advice and suggests methods to help them successfully carry out their tasks. In addition, team leaders often engage in *in vivo supervision,* teaching and supervising interventions in the communities where they are applied.

The team leader is the hub of the wheel, but sometimes the team leader is also a spoke. While the team leader is the direct supervisor for the team, he or she is also a *direct service team member* who spends some time making home visits, accompanying clients to appointments, delivering medications, and so on. The team leader provides services in the same manner that the other members do, but also responds to emergencies and crisis situations. In fact, the team leader is usually the first person called when there is a crisis, whether that crisis has to do with a client (such as an impending hospitalization) or a team member (such as a flat tire that will disrupt the day's schedule of client appointments).

The team leader must be insightful and able to identify and acknowledge the various strengths and passions of the team's members. Some members may be reliably punctual; others may be particularly calm in a crisis or creative with complex problems. Some members may gravitate towards leadership positions; others may be more skilled at articulating a client's point of view; still others excel at the logistics of moving clients into apartments. By accurately assessing an individual's strengths and passions, a team leader can make better, more efficient task assignments.

The team leader has many responsibilities and constantly faces multiple competing demands. In addition to supervising team members, he or she works with the psychiatrist (discussed later) and family physician to oversee the clinical management of the clients. Part hub and part spoke, an effective team leader must be creative, intelligent, organized, ethical, and able to manage stress well by practicing self-care. Since each day holds new challenges and crisis situations, the team leader must be able to think quickly while maintaining a positive team spirit and adhering to the Pathways Housing First philosophy and values.

A day in the life of a team leader

What is a team leader's typical workday like? Perhaps no day is typical, but we asked some of our team leaders to keep a daily log at random. Jen Walker, MSW, team leader at Pathways to Housing Philadelphia, provided us with hers. (Except for Ms. Walker's name, all other names of staff and clients have been changed; clients are referred to by initials only.)

Daily Log: April 6, 2010
Jen Walker, MSW
Team Leader, Pathways to Housing Philadelphia

8:30 a.m.: *As on-call staffer, took two calls before 9:00: PT just wanting to know who was on call; MH needing a ride to the dentist (I called Bob to give him the message).*

9:05 *Arrived at work and discovered that Stan and Trish (service coordinators) who had planned to take RR to court were at the office instead: he hadn't been home when they arrived. I reviewed his file to look up the number for his public defender, which I found and gave to Trish. She called but there was no answer, so I sent her to court to try to prevent a bench warrant.*

9:10 *Facilitated morning meeting. Had lengthy discussion about RC, then rehashed for Dr. C (team psychiatrist), who came late (after another meeting).*

9:45 *During rounds, texted back and forth with Trish about RR as she arrived at court.*

10:10 *Figured out the schedule (assigning list of tasks to staff members); copied and distributed the schedule; told Chelsea (service coordinator) she needs to catch up on progress notes.*

10:20 *Met with housing director for update on HE (no electricity); gave updates on RA and IF.*

10:30 *E-mailed back and forth with Joseph (accountant) about whether certain clients had funds in their accounts, since they had requested more spending money—reviewed my notes from our last meeting and finally got issue resolved.*

10:45 *Trish came back with RR—we talked about what had happened; discussed having him see Dr. C; read his psych eval, reviewed paperwork Trish would have him sign. Talked with her and other staff about whether we can manage his meds every day for three weeks. Then updated Dr. C on the whole situation, introduced him to RR, and sat in for the first minutes of their session.*

11:00 *Helped TH order a Safelink phone on the computer, wrote two docs from April 1.*

11:15 *Chelsea received a call from AL—I listened to the conversation and we talked about options re: check. I e-mailed Stan (clinical director) to ask his advice; he e-mailed back and said he'd call her.*

11:30 *Met with CJ—tokens, cigarettes, talked about apartment. He used phone, I wrote two progress notes from April 1.*

11:45 *Helped Nancy (peer specialist) problem-solve re: taking FO to see apartments. Called Randy G at Pennsylvania Hospital to leave message asking for medication update for FO.*

12:00 *Met with EP for a few minutes; then met with HC for a few minutes and she and Stella (nurse) updated me on some health issues. I wrote two progress notes from 4/1/10.*

12:15 *Helped Bob (ATL from Team 1) decipher some SSI paperwork for one of his clients—trying to determine the protective filing date and how much money the client will get.*

12:30 *Received call from RA—he got into the peer specialist program!*

12:35 *Took a lunch break—still in the office but sat at my desk and ate lunch.*

1:15 *Marcia (program assistant) noted that there were five missing receipts* for the reimbursement—looked through daily schedule book and contact log trying to determine what staffer had used the credit card for what consumer. I asked Marcia to complete that reimbursement without those five receipts. Started this journal and checked e-mail.

1:30   Texted with Trish while she was on a client visit and answered questions re: new apartment for LE and what documents are needed. Talked to housing to find out address of new apartment.

1:40   Nancy called for advice about a sleeping woman on the street who urinated on herself—should she call 911 or city outreach? Advised to call 911.

1:45   Received call from LE. She is not happy with location of new apartment —what can we do? Told her not to panic—we'd work something out.

1:50   Received call from RO about his cable.

1:55   Helped Dr. C use fax machine—told him what documents I needed from him—debated IP's diagnosis.

2:00   Looked at Stella's (nurse's) log from yesterday to determine what times I can bill for since we saw the same people.

2:15   Heard back from Randy G—wrote e-mail to Dr. Raleigh et al re: TO.

2:26   Started the 24 service notes I have to do from yesterday.

2:30   Called Social Security Admin to ask about four problems—got them to release money for three people.

2:45   Researched cable providers for RO.

3:00   Talked to Harry and getting meds poured for AT.

3:15   Received call from BG.

3:30   Wrote more progress notes from yesterday.

4:00   Talked to Bob and told him about how to file to be someone's payee.

4:05   Wrote more progress notes.

4:35   Started talking to DS—she expressed ideations about self-mutilation so I spent half an hour with her.

5:15   Left work.

The Psychiatrist

The psychiatrist has a complex role on the PHF assertive community treatment team. He or she usually functions both as a team member and as the team's medical director. Duties may include initial intake assessments, psychiatric evaluations, medication management, and coordinating crisis assessments with the team. The psychiatrist works closely with all team members because psychiatric input in day-to-day operations is often crucial to the success of a client's treatment. The psychiatrist shares responsibility with the team leader in clinical decision making and also monitors nursing staff or collaborates with the nursing supervisor to ensure that all of a client's medications are dispensed according to best practice guidelines.

The psychiatrist also spends time in the community, often making house calls to see clients and discuss a variety of issues. When hospitalization occurs, the psychiatrist works closely with the inpatient unit psychiatrist, nurses, and other hospital team members to ensure continuity of care and a successful stay. When the client is discharged, the psychiatrist reviews the aftercare plan and discharge summary supplied by the hospital staff. He or she also reviews these orders with the client, and reviews and documents any adjustments in medication dosage and frequency. As noted in chapter 1, the PHF approach adheres to a harm-reduction model. This approach necessitates careful monitoring of psychiatric medications when clients are using substances, so the psychiatrist sees to it that such issues are openly discussed with the clients and other team members.

The psychiatrist, together with the family physician or nurse practitioner (in coordination with the team nurse), also discusses and treats clients' medical conditions. When medical issues arise that cannot be addressed in the community, he or she works with the team to make the necessary appointments for the client to see a primary care physician or an appropriate specialist.

A day in the life of a PHF psychiatrist

Dr. William Tucker of Pathways New York City provided us with a daily journal for a glimpse at a day in the life of a PHF program psychiatrist.

Daily Log: April 7, 2010
William Tucker, M.D.
Psychiatrist, Pathways New York City

8:30 a.m.   *Printed and signed notes written yesterday; filed into Progress Note Binder.*

8:45   *Supervision with psychiatric nurse practitioner, discussing specific cases and education around psychopharmacology and psychotherapy concepts and practices for clients.*

9:15   *Weekly case review with ACT team. Discussed "good news" (rehabilitative gains made by consumers in past week), then discussed clients who have been identified as requiring in-depth clinical discussion by the team, including specific action steps it will take to support consumers. Examples of these clients:*

- *A client who is training to be a peer specialist at Howie the Harp [an advocacy center in Harlem]. Many months of psychoeducation and cognitive behavioral therapy have led him to identify some of his past delusional ideas and hallucinations as a part of a mental health condition that he can modify. He plans to teach a class on managing voices to his peers at Howie the Harp. To decide how and when to disclose his personal experience, he agreed to obtain guidance from the team's peer specialist and assistant team leader.*

- *A client who is under outpatient commitment. We discussed how we will support the consumer and interact with outpatient commitment staff.*

- *A client who shows psychosocial improvements but struggles with poorly maintained diabetes. The team created specific plans to support her with her physical health: a team educated by a nurse and psychiatrist will make structured visits with a diabetic teaching calendar for blood sugar monitoring and management.*

- *A client who, after months of motivational interviewing, is in the late preparation stage of leaving a family member who has been abusive toward her. We discussed ways to help her handle her guilt in leaving her family and clarified her "safety plan" that outlines steps for a safe departure and relocation.*

- *A client with uncontrolled bleeding fibroids who had engaged in medical treatment. The team decided to collaborate more intensively with home health aide, family, and medical providers to support the consumer. Team psychiatrist and nurse educated the team about managing bleeding fibroids, as this related to two other clients as well.*

- *A client recently hospitalized and the team's effective engagement with her while inpatient. The team discussed our interactions with client, inpatient staff, and client's family members in order to ensure her hospitalization is as time-limited as possible and also clinically effective.*

10:45–11:15 *Service Plans (Treatment Plans) reviewed and day planned.*

11:15 *Drove to client's apartment in Queens and discussed vocational plan with a family member of a client who called me while en route.*

11:45 *Met face-to-face with a client in his apartment and provided support-ive psychotherapy. He formally requested to review his chart to "make sure there is no trauma history." This writer collaboratively reviewed his life narrative, clarified his psychosocial history, and used trauma-informed care approaches to educate on how observing a traumatic incident can affect an individual later in life. The client's allopathic medications were lowered and we discussed homeopathic support strategies to support his coping with symptoms.*

12:30 *Drove to client's apartment in Queens.*

1:00 *Met with a client in his apartment to which he recently moved. He discussed his coping with the move, integrating into his new community, and his sense of relief he is no longer harassed by "spirits." We discussed his depression treatment, which has gone from partial response to full remission. Titration of the antidepressant, bupropion, had resulted in decreased nicotine desire and smoking cessation. He received smoking* cessation counseling and expressed plans to continue abstinence from tobacco. He discussed his goals to reconnect with his sons, but he wants to obtain dental work before doing so. We discussed next steps to supporting him on this.

1:50 Drove to another client's apartment. During drive, spoke with team leader and outpatient commitment staff about client recently discussed in case review.

2:30 Met with client and her sons in her apartment for family support interventions, integrated dual disorders treatment, and discussion of harm-reduction strategies to minimize negative consequences of alcohol and substance use. She discussed her future goal to obtain work to do something for herself proactively and as a way to minimize stressors from family relationships. She made specific plans to call a vocational training program and searched the Web site.

3:15 Received call from supported housing team about a client not receiving adequate mental health evaluation while medically hospitalized at local hospital. I called the ACT team and inpatient staff to advocate for psychiatric evaluation and to ensure coordination of care if she is discharged.

3:45 Drove to south Bronx.

4:00 Met with client in his residence to discuss his transition from ACT team to traditional substance use and psychiatric services in the community. He discussed his transition off methadone and goal for abstinence, risks and benefits of engaging in suboxone treatment, and his feelings of loss and change in relationships with team members as he transitions. We explored how feelings about his relationship with family members related to his current transition and support was given.

4:45 Drove to office.

5:30 Faxed documentation to outpatient commitment staff. Documented progress notes of day.

6:45 Ended the workday.

And from Dr. Robert Keisling at Pathways in Washington, DC, we have summaries for two workdays.

Daily Log: April 8 and 9, 2010
Robert Keisling, M.D.
Psychiatrist, Pathways to Housing DC

April 8   *I met with Team 4 today. We have several new patients who have been referred over the past few weeks. Some of them I have not seen. They are still on the street. I have scheduled Tuesday between 10 and noon to do street outreach and see some of these people. One gentleman, a former police officer, is living on the street near the Canadian embassy. He came to the office today and agreed to take a long-acting injectable medication. We have started working with a new pharmacy and are switching everyone over to the bubble pack system, which will relieve the nurses from having to pack meds for our daily and weekly med drop patients. I have a medical student with me on Thursday afternoon and we interviewed several patients.*

April 9   *Morning started with a home visit to see an 80-year-old lady with a 50-year history of mental illness. She has been refusing her meds and has had multiple hospitalizations going back to 1960. Unfortunately she was not there. We checked the local supermarket. Not there either. Will try again on Monday. The rest of the day was spent seeing walk-ins and patients who had regular appointments. The staff took a group of patients to the zoo. I was not able to convince one of our patients to sign up for disability entitlements. He doesn't want to take gov't. money even though the gov't. is paying the rent on his apt. He has been living in the apartment for eighteen months.*

The Family Nurse Practitioner

Meeting clients' physical health concerns is of utmost importance. A 2006 epidemiological study by the National Association of State Mental Health Program Directors[17] reported that, on average, people with severe psychiatric disabilities die twenty-five years earlier than the rest of the population. Many die from treatable ailments such as diabetes, hypertension, and obesity. Given the population served by the PHF program, it is an ethical and clinical imperative to treat these and other medical problems. That is why the PHF assertive community treatment team includes a family physician or nurse practitioner (NP) in any manner possible—directly as part of the team or through a collaborative agreement with another entity. (A registered nurse, physician's assistant, or internist could also fill this position. Again, if funding or other practical constraints preclude hiring directly for this position, the team must have strong linkages to primary care providers.)

The NP participates in some of the morning meetings and case review conferences. The NP provides comprehensive and holistic primary care, including physical exams, diagnosis development, and acute and chronic illness management. In collaboration with the family physician and other medical staff on the team, the NP can often prescribe and evaluate pharmacological care and conduct in-home initial health screenings. Since many PHF clients do not regularly see a medical doctor and are reluctant to receive any kind of medical treatment, the NP must match the treatment level and schedule to the client's comfort level and need. Fortunately, because of the flexible structure and client-centered approach of the PHF ACT model, it is possible for physical exams to take place over the course of many meetings if necessary.

The NP can also provide nutritional counseling, teach classes on healthy cooking, and lead smoking cessation groups. He or she can also organize walking groups and coordinate peer support groups for those clients who struggle with similar medical problems.

The Nurse

One of the nurse's chief responsibilities is to review all client intake documentation and create a medical focus list. This list places high priority on clients with known medical ailments who are not currently receiving treatment, clients with unknown medical histories, and high-risk clients (such as elderly clients, heavy smokers, those with a history of substance use, those who engage in high-risk sexual practices, and morbidly obese clients).

Immediately after reviewing the documentation, the nurse schedules visits with each client to begin the engagement process and to encourage clients to take advantage of available medical treatment. These visits do not have to feel like medical interventions. For example, the nurse might first meet with a client at a coffee shop for a casual conversation. It sometimes is possible to help someone move in and set up an apartment without any discussion of treatment at all.

The nurse must be comfortable developing a rapport with clients, because doing so helps establish a positive, noninvasive relationship that can build trust. This often results in a client's sincere willingness to address medical issues. However, even if a client consistently resists addressing medical issues, the nurse continues the engagement process and informs the client that he or she is available as a physical and mental health resource.

Most interactions between the nurse and a client occur in the client's apartment. This home visit is an ideal time for the nurse to assess the client's environment, including basic hygiene, nutrition, and physical safety level. For example, if the nurse observes that the client does not have any food in the refrigerator but *does* have a lot of trash from fast-food restaurants, the nurse might choose to discuss the importance of healthy eating and might even accompany the client to the grocery store to purchase food. During the home visit, the nurse also assesses the potential need for home health amenities such as shower chairs, handrails, raised toilet seats, or prosthetic aids. This type of assessment is especially important for elderly or physically disabled clients. When a team includes an occupational therapist, it is ideal for the nurse to interface with that person and develop a plan that best supports those clients with disabilities.

The nurse also escorts clients to medical appointments if they want or need this type of support (other team members assist with this as well). Accompanying a client to an appointment is a great opportunity to engage with the client and interface with other medical specialists who provide care. During medical appointments, the nurse can help the client understand the purpose of the appointment and explain the doctor's report and recommendations. The nurse can advocate for clients by helping them understand and express their treatment options. If a client is hospitalized, the nurse, along with other team members, visits the client as frequently as possible, assuring the person that the program has not forgotten him or her. While the client remains in the hospital, the nurse speaks with hospital staff to ensure continuity of care and the appropriate level of treatment.

Equally important is the nurse's coordination and management of the client's psychiatric medication regimens. This requires a very close working relationship with the team psychiatrist. The nurse and psychiatrist work together to ensure the proper administration and distribution of medication. Nurses are in more frequent contact with clients and can report signs of distressing medication side effects, noncompliance, and positive and adverse reactions to medication.

The nurse is also a teacher who helps educate team members about clients' medication needs. In this way, the nurse helps prioritize work with clients who have medication needs and helps team members work with clients so clients can ultimately self-administer their own medications.

The Peer Specialist

The peer specialist is essential to the team's success because he or she provides wise counsel from someone who has "been there, done that." The presence of a peer specialist on the team directly demonstrates to other team members and to clients that recovery is indeed possible. The fact that a person who has been diagnosed with a severe mental illness—just like the clients the team now serves—is now an active and productive member of the team, provides a powerful, positive, and inspiring example. The peer specialist proves that recovery is not just a philosophy or a theory; it is a lived experience.

Since peer specialists usually have a profound understanding of their own recovery process, they are often very actively involved in the recovery community. The peer specialist is thus an excellent resource for client referrals to self-help and other support groups and is a sought-after educator or group facilitator to help other clients learn the skills necessary to support their own recovery. Peer specialists are especially well suited to teach the "toolkit" for Illness Management and Recovery (known in some places as its friendly parallel, Wellness Management and Recovery). The peer specialist can also help clients develop Wellness Recovery Action Plans. (These WRAPS are discussed in more detail in chapter 7.)

Peer specialists have been on both sides of the team's work, so they are in a good position to help ensure that the team is operating from a client-centered, recovery-focused approach. In addition, peer specialists frequently describe how clients may view the team's intervention, an invaluable insight.

Peer specialists can offer a wealth of information about resources in the recovery community as well as in the team's larger community. The peer often garners a client's trust, creating hope in the possibility of recovery in ways that other team members simply cannot.

The presence of a peer on the PHF ACT team helps team members and clients consistently challenge their own assumptions about how much recovery is possible. Peer specialists effectively blur the line between who provides services and who receives them. The teams with peer specialists are at less risk for relapse into a medical model practice, referring to clients by their diagnosis and in other explicit and subtle ways resorting back to an "us and them" clinical culture. The peer specialist's presence summons all to regularly consider some fundamental questions and observations about a diagnosis of mental illness and its place in a human life. Peers on a team bring to mind one of psychiatrist Harry Stack Sullivan's core observations: "We are all much more simply human than otherwise, be we happy and successful, contented and detached, miserable and mentally disordered, or whatever."

A day in the life of a peer specialist

Jerome Marzan offered us two diary entries. Jerome is a peer specialist, but his official job title is assistant team leader at Pathways New York City.

Daily Log: April 6 and 7, 2010
Jerome Marzan
Assistant Team Leader, Pathways New York City

April 6

9:00–10:00 a.m. *Worked on incident report.*

10:00–11:00 *Assisted client in locating detox facility. Client is afraid to return to his apartment because he was attacked by four men inside his apartment a week ago. The men were associates of his brother. Client denies using any illegal drugs. Hasn't paid rent in months.*

He requested assistance in going to a detox, but says he doesn't have a drug problem. He stated he will drink a beer to get admitted. He is also a veteran. I contacted VA hospital and made a referral. He was admitted later that day. (1) He is in a safe place and is receiving help. (2) Through lab reports from detox, the team will find out if he is using any illegal drugs and can develop a plan of action to address a problem. (3) He agreed to allow Pathways to become his payee to prevent eviction. (4) He will begin to develop a more trusting relationship with team.

11:00–12:30 *Apartment visit inspection*

12:30–1:30 *Lunch*

1:30–2:00 *Provided client with money management services. He only receives $68.50 every two weeks from Public Assistance. He is expecting to become a father in a couple of months. I assisted him in exploring his options to get a job or attend a vocational training school that has job placement and also to meet with Pathways employment specialist.*

2:00–2:30 *Followed up with phone call to parole officer and social worker at hospital and was able to give them a good report. However, I spoke to another parole officer who is ready to violate client and place him in jail. I advocated for treatment instead of incarceration. Parole officer was willing to give him a second chance.*

2:30–3:00 *Assisted client in adding new goal to service plan. She had moved into her apartment ten months ago. When she was admitted into the program she stated she only has two goals: (1) to maintain her apartment and (2) to reconnect with her family. Today I assisted her in exploring something positive that she would like to do or something she has done in the past that she would like to do again. She expressed her interest in learning about computers. I discussed with her the availability of classes that we have at the Resource Center. She stated she would start attending. This new goal has been added to her service plan. Team will encourage and remind her about the* classes. *If she doesn't make it to the class within the first couple of weeks, the team will offer to pick her up and accompany her to the first computer class as an additional support.*

3:00–5:00 *Paperwork*

April 7

9:00–10:00 a.m. *Morning meeting.*

10:00–11:00 *Provided supervision and training to new service coordinator.*

11:00–12:00 *Provided clients with individual wellness self-management services.*

12:00–1:00 *Lunch*

1:00–2:00 *Provided client with individual substance abuse counseling. He is a heavy IV cocaine and heroin user who recently lost his Medicaid benefits. The good news is that he's not in denial and is willing to get help. The bad news is he has no health insurance. No insurance means no inpatient detox or rehab services will accept him. Now there is a certain city hospital that will accept someone into detox without Medicaid. He was admitted to Bellevue for a few days and discharged. He needs longer treatment: rehab for 21 days. For rehab, there is a federal grant for programs to accept people without Medicad. Bronx State Hospital is one of them. However you need a lot of documentation, like a psych evaluation, psychosocial, physical, and PPD [tuberculosis] testing. Progress has been made. I completed the psychosocial, Dr. D. did the psych evaluation, our LPN did the physical, but we ran out of medicine for the PPD test. We should receive it on Tuesday. The main element in providing services is to KEEP HOPE ALIVE!*

2:00–5:00 *Office coverage*

The Family Specialist

Working with the client from a family systems perspective, the team's family specialist considers the client's familial, support, and other networks. This person's goal is to work with clients who choose to improve and restore their relationships with relatives. When the client wishes it, the family specialist convenes meetings with the client's family and assists in any reconnection or reconciliation process. If family members tend to misconstrue a client's negative behavior as directed at them, the family specialist often helps them understand it more as a symptom of the client's own suffering. He or she is responsible for working with the client to formulate and realize family-related goals. By serving as the catalyst for a client to reconnect with loved ones, the family specialist can help create an event that can play a major role in a client's recovery journey.

The Wellness Management and Recovery Specialist

The Wellness Management and Recovery (WMR) specialist is trained in the evidence-based practice known as Illness Management and Recovery.[18] (As noted previously, these terms are interchangeable; they differ only in tone.) This specialist helps clients identify what recovery would mean for their specific life experience. He or she helps clients see how their current behaviors relate to their recovery goal and to explore what hurdles might be standing in the way.

Because the PHF ACT team is dedicated to the principles of recovery, the team's day-to-day environment is particularly well suited for this approach. The WMR (IMR) program is generally conducted one-to-one, through a series of individual appointments with clients who have expressed interest. This specialist helps clients develop strategies to feel less isolated, provides education about relationships, and teaches relaxation and meditation techniques. Together with the nurse, peer specialist, or other team members, this specialist often facilitates a number of groups, such as a walking group, an exercise group, a smoking cessation program, and a nutrition and healthy cooking class.

Because clients are often more interested in their medical health than their psychiatric condition, health and wellness groups can help build and strengthen trusting relationships. They can also offer opportunities to discuss other avenues of recovery. Additionally, because psychiatric medications usually have multiple medical side effects, including diabetes and obesity, the wellness management specialist promotes—and makes accessible—exercise and nutrition groups.

The Supported Employment Specialist

Another SAMHSA evidence-based practice is known by two names: Individual Placement and Support (IPS) and Supported Employment, or SE (the term used here).[19] This practice is highly compatible with Pathways' values, mission, and operation. While new clients name housing as their top priority—whether or not they suffer from a psychiatric disability—"a job" is often the second thing they name. Supported Employment offers the most effective way to help clients get and keep a job. SE operates on the principle that every individual, regardless of abilities, has the right to learn, work, and contribute to his or her community. Similarly, every individual has the right to seek an education and to find meaningful employment that will improve his or her quality of life.

The SE process has no lengthy assessments, no transitional employment or training period. The only question needed to begin it is "Do you want a job?" If the answer is affirmative, the client and the SE specialist begin to plan the steps needed to achieve this goal. The SE specialist teaches, guides, and coaches clients as they write résumés, search for jobs, prepare for interviews, find transportation to and from work, undergo training, adjust to a work schedule, and accept new responsibilities. The SE specialist can help identify career paths, meaningful jobs, negotiate accommodations with employers, and serve as a liaison or support between the clients and their employers.

One of the greatest concerns for clients is how full- or part-time employment will affect their government entitlements. This concern is less about the financial implications than it is about the medical insurance benefit tied to these entitlements. Clients who are taking a lot of medication cannot afford to lose their insurance. To address this and other related issues, the SE specialist is highly conversant with the rules and conditions of the various benefit and entitlement payments and can address clients' concerns in individual or group workshop sessions. The SE specialist also updates other team members about these workshops and any changes in benefit rules and regulations.

The most effective teams do not rely on one SE specialist to accomplish all that must be done for clients to choose, get, and keep employment. The entire PHF ACT team must be involved and committed to helping clients find employment. *"Work is everybody's business"* is a PHF slogan that captures the need for every team member to make employment a high priority—especially because it is a high priority for clients.

Although some clients fear losing their benefits, others fear that they may not succeed in the job market. For staff working with such clients, Motivational Interviewing and a Stages of Change model can be very useful. (See chapter 7 for more details.) These approaches will help the client identify his or her ambivalence about work and help the team understand what might be the logical next step for a particular client.

The SE specialist plays a key role in a recovery-oriented practice because he or she helps clients articulate and realize their goals in the areas of work, school, and career. Employment is about beginning to get out of poverty and achieving a standard of living above entitlements, and it also has enormous psychological meaning. The self-definition of a client with psychiatric disabilities changes from a person with disabilities to a person with abilities. The social roles defined by employment open up entirely new worlds of socialization and possibilities for social inclusion. The transformation from client to employee is not only a change of employment status—it is also a change of self-definition and social status. The SE specialist encourages and assists clients to look for employment that aligns with personal interests and goals.

Perhaps most importantly, the SE specialist can help clients redefine themselves as working, contributing members of society. That is what recovery is about.

The Substance Abuse Specialist

The substance abuse specialist uses the principles of integrated dual disorders treatment (IDDT) to help clients manage and reduce their addictions. IDDT is another SAMHSA evidence-based mental health approach for treating individuals with co-occurring disorders, most commonly mental illness and substance abuse.[20] In a PHF program, this specialist visits those clients who, at their intake assessment, have reported a history of alcohol or other drug use. The IDDT model follows the harm-reduction approach, which means the substance abuse specialist does not require clients to obtain treatment for their addiction to alcohol or other drugs. The substance abuse specialist does, however, visit with clients to determine the stage of their use and their awareness or insight into the extent of their use. The team needs to determine whether clients are actively engaged in substance use or abuse, and to also determine whether they are in denial, the "pre-contemplation" stage of change, or perhaps even contemplating treatment. (Again, see chapter 7 for more details on these Stages of Change).

The substance abuse specialist consults with other team members to determine the best course of action for each client. When a client decides to pursue a treatment option, the specialist offers support in the form of counseling (in group and individual settings) that is based on the harm-reduction model. The substance abuse specialist also educates team members so that they can more effectively help clients who are coping with substance abuse and mental health concerns.

The Program Assistant

The program assistant has many responsibilities. He or she plays a vital role in the morning meeting, for example. The assistant updates charts and generally keeps the ACT team's paperwork organized. The program assistant is frequently the first person to greet clients when they come to the office and is therefore responsible for creating a welcoming and safe environment. He or she also handles petty cash disbursements and other program supplies. Often, the assistant helps the team disburse clients' entitlement benefits, organizes travel, and supports the team in a number of ways.

The ACT Team's Morning Meeting

For the ACT team in the Pathways setting, the purpose of the daily morning meeting is for the team to share clinical information relevant to supporting a client's achievement of his or her goals. The team is rarely all together except during the morning meeting, so it is essential that *all* team members, including the administrative assistant, attend. A great deal of information is shared during the meeting. Every single client (about seventy-five clients, for most teams) is reviewed, even if very briefly. Services to be provided to each client are discussed, and the daily schedule is planned, indicating who will provide what services to which clients. All of this must be accomplished in forty-five to sixty minutes. Team members must be focused and actively listening participants, and the entire team must perform as a cohesive and highly efficient group.

The origins of the ACT team morning meeting can be traced back to the psychiatric hospital morning rounds. Even before Drs. Test, Stein, and Marx had the good sense to de-institutionalize the staff and bring them out into the community, the interdisciplinary staff of the wards met regularly to discuss *each and every client* on their ward.[21] They read the notes from the previous day and planned their interventions for the day ahead. After the morning rounds, the staff left the conference room and entered the ward to interact with their patients.

Today in the PHF program, ACT teams meet every morning in a conference room of the team's offices located in one of the city's affordable housing neighborhoods to quickly discuss the work to be done with *each and every client*. Notes are read and plans are made. After the morning meeting, the team members leave the conference room and begin to visit their clients who are living in their own apartments in the surrounding neighborhood. Although some of the structures of the morning meeting resemble those of morning rounds, the treatment philosophy of the teams and the living conditions of the clients have evolved from a medical model to a recovery model.

The function of the meeting is to ensure that each team member has the most current information about clients' needs and goals. This is crucial because there are no individualized caseloads: all team members are expected to provide services to any client who is served by their team. Each morning, anywhere from sixty to a hundred client situations must be discussed in less than an hour, so the meeting must remain highly focused at all times. If team members are not performing one of the several tasks that are required to run the meeting (reading notes, studying electronic charts or records, viewing the contact log, or writing on the board), they are actively listening and looking for ways to be helpful. In these meetings, the language used is brief, precise, and goal-focused. If an issue arises that is too complicated to resolve during the morning meeting, it is tabled until after the meeting.

It is essential that a quick and efficient tempo be maintained throughout the meeting to complete the many tasks facing the team. The morning meeting conference room has the aura of an operating room or airport control tower. Everyone must focus on the information being discussed. Cell phones are turned off (except for the on-call phone). Every team member is actively involved in every aspect of the meeting, and no other work takes place during the meeting.

The goals of the ACT morning meeting are to

- review every client served by the team

- note significant interactions that have occurred since the last meeting

- discuss necessary follow-ups

- create a schedule for that day

- update the weekly plan

- update the monthly plan

- share information and maintain transparency

Because the morning meeting is central to the team's operation, it is worth taking time here to provide a clear description of the meeting and to identify key terms, describe some of the forms used to run the meeting, and provide a list of the preparatory and administrative tasks. This is accomplished using the boards and logs method as the illustrative example. For teams that use software programs to review clinical information and plan their schedules during the morning meeting, the description presented here is still useful as a cross-check to ensure your software system includes all the information you need to run your meeting effectively.

This section is not about presenting an evidence-based practice. It is about ensuring that your ACT team conducts an effective morning meeting, that all of the information needed at the meeting is readily available, and that the team can efficiently conduct the meeting and plan the day in about an hour's time. Ultimately, the meeting's purpose is to achieve the best possible client outcomes. Thus, the effectiveness of any morning meeting system is really best assessed by considering whether the team's clients are achieving their goals.

Table 1, Quick Questions and Answers, summarizes the who, why, what, when, where, and how of the meeting. Table 2, Key Terms Explained, explains both the vocabulary and the forms used in the meeting, such as the on-call log, the goal board, and the daily schedule.

Table 1
The ACT Team Meeting: Quick Questions and Answers

Who attends the meeting?	All team members:
	team leader
	psychiatrist
	nurse
	nurse practitioner
	peer specialist
	family systems specialist (optional)
	wellness management specialist
	occupational therapist (optional)
	Supported Employment specialist
	substance abuse specialist
	program assistant
Why is the meeting held?	To keep all team members informed and on task
What is discussed?	Clients' daily progress
When is it held?	Every morning at 9 a.m.
Where is the meeting held?	In the ACT conference room at the program office
How long does the meeting last?	One hour

Table 2

The ACT Team Meeting: Key Terms Explained

Contact Log	This three-ring binder contains alphabetized contact sheets, one for each client.
Contact Sheets	Contact sheets make up the contents of the Contact Log. Each client's contact sheet covers one month at a time. At the end of each month each client gets a new sheet for the new month. Contact sheets contain • basic demographic information • the date of last contact with the client • what service was performed on that date • which team member provided the service • a summarized update
Progress Notes	These are the clinical progress notes written after contacts with clients or after meetings with people who play a key role in a client's life. A separate binder can contain these notes, or they may be placed in the contact log behind each client's contact sheet. A system must be created that ensures every progress note is filed in each client's chart/medical record every day. Team members can hold on to their notes so they can read them during the meeting. After the meeting, team members should immediately file their notes, or give them to the program assistant to file.
Dry-Erase Boards	At least three dry-erase boards are kept on the conference room walls: the weekly schedule board, the monthly schedule board, and the clients' goal board. During the meeting, these boards are filled in with information. They are large—4 by 6 feet is recommended—and displayed in clear view.

Weekly Schedule Board	The **weekly schedule board** tracks
	
	• the team's schedule of appointments with clients this week (including appointments that clients have scheduled and requested a team member to accompany them)
	• the staff schedule
	   • where each staff member will be (i.e., covering the office, out doing home visits in a certain section of the city) and who is on call
	   • who is away on vacation or out that day

Monthly Schedule Board	The **monthly schedule board** tracks • appointments and events scheduled beyond the present week, which helps the team look forward into the upcoming month
Goal Board	The **goal board** lists • all the clients' names • all of the clients' current goals

On-Call Log	The designated on-call team member carries this three-ring binder and records all on-call activity in it. At the end of that person's on-call shift (usually one week), he or she passes the log to the next on-call person.

The on-call log contains emergency information such as

- phone numbers for landlords or building superintendents
- phone numbers for locksmiths
- contact information for team leaders and supervisors (cell phone numbers, pagers, and so on)

The on-call log records

- all calls that the on-call person receives
- the caller's name
- the time of the call
- the reason for the call
- the response or action taken and whether it meets the criteria to be designated an "incident"

All on-call activity is reported each morning to the entire team. (However, whenever the on-call person wants guidance when handling a call, he or she should alert the team leader or on-call supervisor immediately, rather than waiting until the morning meeting.)

Programs that choose to go paperless (see Electronic Alternatives, below) may require staffers to keep a laptop with them while on call. This ensures that the staff has access to the client's most recent progress notes and to all relevant information about the client in the event of an emergency (such as emergency contact numbers, the client's crisis plan, and so on).

Daily Assignment Sheet/Daily Schedule	This is compiled during the morning meeting, often on computer by the program assistant. The assignments consist of

- appointments
- home visits scheduled for that day
- new appointments or home visits scheduled as the result of information shared during the morning meeting

Everyone receives a copy of the daily schedule at the end of the meeting.

Daily Visit Schedule	This schedule lists all the visits (home, community, and office) that need to happen on the day of the morning meeting.

Electronic Alternatives	Some programs may choose to run a paperless program in which all schedules, progress notes, assessments, and plans are stored in a database.

In many Canadian provinces, family physicians are required to use an Electronic Medical Record, and programs may wish to have all of their staff use the same system to ensure that all team members have access to all of the progress notes in a centralized area. Other programs, however, may choose to use Case Management Software in addition to a traditional Electronic Medical Record.

Sample Forms for ACT Team Use

The various forms, sheets, and schedules mentioned in tables 1 and 2 can be created by program staff. The following annotated examples can serve as models. (See also appendix C-1 for related information.)

Sample Client Contact Sheet

Client name: John Doe
Month: September 2009

Col. 1	Col. 2	Col. 3	Col. 4	Col. 5	Col. 6	Col. 7	Col. 8	Col. 9
Date	In Person, in the Office	In Person, in the Field	Collateral	On the Phone	Progress Note Written	Date of Follow-Up	Contact Person	Summary
9/1								
9/2								
9/3								
(And so on—this form will have 30 rows.)								

Notes:

Column 1: All dates of the current month appear here (this sheet will have 30 rows).

Columns 2–5: These show the types of contact the team may have with the client (or with other key people in the client's life, known as "collateral"). Staff check these columns to show what kind of contact occurred.

Column 6: Staff check this column if a progress note has been written that day.

Column 7: Staffer enters the date of the follow-up contact.

Column 8: The staffer who had contact with the client writes his or her name here. (This person is also responsible for writing a progress note, if needed. The completed note *must* be placed either in a progress note binder or behind the client's contact sheet. This should all be done *before* the morning meeting.)

Column 9: Here, staff summarize and/or update data and the client's corresponding plan, based on information from the morning meeting. This update includes the next time a team member will see the client, and the activity to take place on that date. All of this material—the most recent progress note, the next scheduled visit, and what will occur during that visit—is reviewed during the morning meeting. (This column should be wider to allow for more detail.)

Sample Weekly Schedule (on Dry-Erase Board)

Clients are identified by initials; staff by first names.   **Appts=Appointments**   **HV=Home Visit**

	Monday	Tuesday	Wednesday	Thursday	Friday	Saturday/ Sunday	Team member on call	Clients in hospital or jail
Clients needing medication assistance	Meds: JK, LM	Meds: ST, AV, FO	Meds: BV needs IM injection				Jake: week of 9/21–9/28	PS: 9/19, Mercy Hospital, voluntary
Staff in office (with program assistant)	Jules	Erik	Sam	Lavelle	Darlene			
9–10 a.m.	Morning meeting	Morning meeting	Morning meeting	Morning meeting	Morning meeting			
10–12 noon	Appts: HV:	Appts: HV: MP, LW, MK	Appts: Appts: 10:45 a.m.: KP to dentist	Appts: HV:	Appts: HV:			
12 noon– 2 p.m.	Appts: HV:	Appts: HV:	Appts: HV:	Appts: 12–1:30: Harm Reduction Group	Appts: HV:			
2–4 p.m.	Appts: HV:	Appts: 2-4: Weekly Case Conference Mtg	Appts: HV:	Appts: HV:	Appts: HV:			
4–6 p.m.	Appts: HV:	Appts: HV:	Appts: HV:	Appts: HV:	Appts: HV:			
6–8 p.m.	Appts:	Appts:	Appts:	Appts:	Appts:			

Notes:

Every weekday, morning meeting is held from 9 to 10 a.m. Saturday and Sunday morning meetings are less formal (fewer staff; more flexible timing).

This schedule is revised continuously. On Wednesday, the past Monday and Tuesday notations are erased and replaced by the Monday and Tuesday of the upcoming week; similar updates are made each subsequent day. Relevant information from the monthly schedule is also transferred onto this board.

Sample Monthly Schedule (on Dry-Erase Board)

September 2009

Monday	Tuesday	Wednesday	Thursday	Friday	Saturday	Sunday
	1	2	3	4	5	6
7	8	9	PM: Court 10	11	12	13
14	JW: CAT scan, 1:30 15	16	17	18	19	20
21	22	23	24	MK: Job interview, 2 p.m. 25	26	27
28	29	30				

Notes:

This board essentially represents a one-month calendar.

Client appointments and other key dates are added throughout the month.

Sample Goal Board (on Dry-Erase Board)

Client	Current Goal	Date Initiated
LP	Obtain new dentures	9/1/09
SG	Sign up for online dating	9/5/09
FS	Go to OB/GYN	9/8/09
PC	Obtain a job	9/6/09
FG	Reduce my drinking on the weekends	9/4/09
PM	Take my daughter to lunch	9/5/09

Sample On-Call Log

On-Call Log: East Harlem ACT Team

Date: Sept. 22–23, 2009

Name of Client	Time of Call	Reason for Call	Response/ Action	Was an incident report completed?
DP	1 a.m.	Toilet jammed	Told her we would talk to the building super ASAP	No

Sample Daily Activity Schedule

Daily Activity Schedule: East Harlem ACT Team

Date: Tuesday, Sept. 22, 2009

Name of Client	Activity, Time, and Location	Team member	Goal	Stage of Change (SOC)
LP	Home visit: 12 noon, 8th and Locust	Jared	To see her dentist	Preparation
SG	Eye doctor appt. (meet at client's home, 1:30 p.m.)	Kristen	Obtain glasses	Action

Notes:

In right-hand column, clients are identified by a phase in the Stages of Change model.

A Hypothetical Morning Meeting

This PHF ACT morning meeting begins promptly at nine o'clock, with all team members present. Everyone is already seated and ready to begin. To ensure a smooth-running meeting, the following tasks have been preassigned before each meeting:

Task	Team member assigned
Read progress notes aloud as needed	All team members write progress notes
Read the contact log aloud	Mary
Update the weekly and monthly schedules (on dry-erase boards)	Steve
Compile the daily schedule	Theresa, on computer
Read the on-call log aloud	Max, who was on call the night before the meeting

Mary begins reading client names from the contact log. After each name is read, team members read aloud from their progress notes if they feel it is necessary. It should take just ten to fifteen seconds to review each client's activity. For example:

Mary (reading from contact log): "Frank Dodge."

Edward, the SE specialist (reading from his progress notes): "Frank applied for a job at a shoe store yesterday and has an interview scheduled for Thursday."

Sherri, the nurse: "Frank has a dentist appointment today at 3:00."

Steve, who is managing the two dry-erase boards, updates them to reflect Frank's upcoming interview and appointment.

Theresa, who is in charge of the daily schedule, transcribes this information about Frank's dentist appointment into the day's schedule.

Throughout the meeting, Steve and Theresa continue to update the boards and daily schedule as team members provide new information about each client that Mary names.

After all the names from the contact log have been read and commented on, the on-call log is read aloud by whoever was on duty the previous night. In the example below, Max the psychiatrist was the team member on call.

> Max: "Doris called at 1 a.m. to say her toilet was backed up. I told her someone would come over this morning to look at it."

This new information is duly recorded by Steve on the dry-erase boards and by Theresa in the daily schedule.

The meeting continues until the on-call log has been read and team members have given their updates. The meeting adjourns at ten o'clock.

Immediately after the meeting, the program assistant prints the Daily Schedule and each team member receives a copy. With this in hand, everyone is aware of everyone else's schedule, which allows transparency and openness. By sharing information in this way, team members in the field who need assistance will know who is close by and available. Using this schedule, the team leader or assistant team leader helps team members prioritize their visits. Team members should remain in close communication during most of the day.

The ACT Weekly Case Conference

In addition to the morning meeting, PHF ACT team members participate in a weekly case conference, which typically lasts about two hours and focuses on the clinical needs of the clients. One purpose of this weekly meeting is to review clients' progress and update the goal planning for the treatment plan. The weekly case review also allows for long-term planning.

Chapter 5 Summary

Assertive community treatment (ACT) is a well-documented approach for treating those with serious and persistent mental illnesses. In this model, a multidisciplinary team delivers a full range of medical, psychosocial, and rehabilitative services to clients in a *community*—rather than institutional—setting.

These are some of the key features of the ACT approach:

- interdisciplinary staffing that includes expertise in psychiatry, nursing, social work, vocational functioning, substance abuse treatment, and related fields

- team approach (shared caseloads and daily team meetings)

- low staff-client ratios (one staff person for ten clients)

- locus of contact in the community

- intensive and frequent contacts with clients

- assertive outreach

- focus on symptom management and everyday problems

- ready access in times of crisis (twenty-four-hour availability)

- time-unlimited services

The boards and logs method is a widely used method for keeping track of team and client data and scheduling staff time; electronic tracking methods are also possible.

In the PHF context, the purpose of the **ACT team's daily morning meeting** is to ensure that each team member has the most current information about clients' needs and goals. With no individualized caseloads, all team members are expected to provide services to any client served by their team.

Goals of the morning meeting are to complete these tasks efficiently:

- review every client in the PHF program

- note significant interactions that have occurred since the last meeting

- discuss necessary follow-up

- create a schedule for that day

- update the weekly plan

- update the monthly plan

- share information and maintain transparency

Chapter 6

The PHF Intensive Case Management Team

THIS CHAPTER DESCRIBES THE STRENGTHS MODEL of services offered by the PHF intensive case management (ICM) team. It also describes the ICM team structure and staff roles and the weekly team meeting.

The ICM Strengths Model of Service Delivery

> *[In the strengths model] A 'radiating effect' occurs. It's as if by focusing on a single strength, the strong part of the self begins to radiate outward, building a new life of meaning and purpose.*
>
> —Patricia Deegan, foreword to *The Strengths Model* by
> Charles A. Rapp and Richard J. Goscha

At Pathways Housing First, the ICM team offers a coordinated and brokered approach that delivers services based on the strengths model of services. This model employs six principles outlined by Dr. Charles Rapp in the foundational text he coauthored with Richard Goscha, *The Strengths Model: Case Management with People with Psychiatric Disabilities* (second edition, 2006). These principles have been cited extensively in numerous articles about case management:

1. People with psychiatric disabilities can recover, reclaim, and transform their lives.

2. It is important to focus on an individual's strengths.

3. The community is viewed as an oasis of resources, not as a barrier.

4. The client is the director of the helping process.

5. The case manager–client relationship is primary and essential.

6. The primary setting for the work is in the community.

These principles are in complete alignment with the principles of recovery embraced by PHF. The services coordinated and brokered with outside providers include family and community integration, crisis intervention, mental health and substance abuse integrated treatment, medical care, vocational and educational counseling, and any other support requested by the individual. Interagency cooperation is essential in the ICM approach, so delivery of services and strong connections must be built across multiple systems to ensure continuity of care.

These points succinctly describe the ICM model of service and support in the context of Pathways Housing First.

- ICM services, like ACT services, are client-driven and based on the client's strengths and interests.

- ICM teams typically use an independent practitioner model in which one staff member is responsible for a certain number of clients. The PHF ICM team uses a modified version of this arrangement. While each team member is primarily responsible for the work and charting for ten to twenty clients, the team members also become familiar with each other's clients and can substitute for each other when the need arises.

- ICM staff-to-client ratios range from 1:10 to 1:20, depending on severity of clients' needs.

- ICM services are available to the client five days a week, and an ICM is on call by telephone 24/7. The on-call responsibilities rotate among team members, so having familiarity and experience with the team's entire roster of clients allows the on-call member to provide a personalized response.

- ICM is not a direct service model; it is a brokerage of services model. Clients are offered a full range of treatment and support services, but some of the services are performed by the team and others by community agencies. Team members offer help in such areas as budgeting, cleaning, food preparation, laundry, and connecting with spiritual, medical, and other services or institutions in the community.

- ICM teams ensure the coordination of care and services.

- ICM team members teach and encourage clients to advocate for themselves in seeking needed services; they also advocate for their clients when asked to do so. ICM teams establish relationships with community providers, seek out natural supports in their clients' community, and navigate the benefits and entitlements bureaucracies.

- ICM teams provide housing support and work to prevent eviction and re-hospitalization.

- ICM is flexible and client-determined.

- Services provided by the ICM team do not have a predetermined time limit. Typically, a client uses fewer and fewer services as time goes by until the client and the team determine that services are no longer needed. At that point, the client is discharged from the roster. Being discharged in no way affects that client's housing status. The client gets to stay in his or her apartment with his or her rent subsidy after the services are no longer needed.

- ICM teams make frequent house calls or provide services in the community. ICM team members usually visit frequently when a client initially moves into an apartment, but once a client is settled, the average number of visits is two per month. (This number is flexible; some clients require weekly visits while others are seen once a month at home and once a month at the office.) A crisis, a client's refusal of a visit, or a client who is seldom home when the team visits—any of these is a signal to review the work with this client and immediately increase the number of visits until stability is restored. Visits are also made on an as-needed basis or when directed by the client.

• Last but not least, ICM teams must hold out hope at all times.

The ICM Team Members

The intensive case management team is composed of the following members:

- Team leader (Some teams also have an assistant team leader.)

- Intensive case managers (These team members may be trained as social workers, nurses, or substance abuse specialists, or they are individuals with degrees in the human services who have years of clinical experience. Including peer specialists as part of the staff is also highly recommended.) All team members work as "intensive case managers," not as specialists.

- Program assistant

As mentioned, ICM teams traditionally broker services to outside agencies. Although they are not required to do so, ICM teams in the PHF setting are encouraged to have a part-time psychiatric nurse practitioner or psychiatrist.

Although the ICM team does not have the same breadth of specialties that the ACT team has, clients who receive ICM services are not limited to certain types or frequency of services. On the contrary, clients have access to a full complement of treatment services, but outside agencies usually provide them.

The Team Leader

At Pathways Housing First, the ICM team leader provides philosophical and clinical direction, organizes team work schedules, provides clinical supervision regarding every client, offers one-on-one supervision with team members as well as in-the-field leadership, and serves as the liaison between administration and the team. The team leader knows ICM theory and has the ability to implement the strengths-based approach to ICM services. The team leader ensures that all documentation for treatment planning and progress notes is complete and up to date. He or she understands the PHF model of service, knows the regulatory requirements of the program's funding agencies and licensing bodies, and is also familiar with legislation that pertains to PHF clients.

As a clinical supervisor, the team leader helps the other team members develop skills and techniques needed to provide recovery-focused services, to handle crises, and to ensure the brokerage of all needed services. He or she also works with team members on ways to develop a positive, forward-looking rapport with clients. By virtue of a strong command of community resources related to health, mental health, addiction, income support, and housing, the team leader can help team members when they face particularly challenging situations.

The team leader must be aware of his or her role as a mentor to the other team members. In this capacity, the team leader meets with team members for individual supervision for an hour every two weeks. Team members are encouraged to bring to this meeting any examples of specific cases or situations with which they need assistance. The team leader offers perspective, advice, and methods that can help the team member succeed.

While the team leader is the direct supervisor for the team, he or she is also a direct service team member, spending at least half the time making home visits, accompanying clients to appointments, delivering medications, etc. The team leader provides services in the same manner as the other team members do and responds to emergencies and crises. Unlike the PHF ACT team leader, the ICM team leader does not have the luxury of a daily morning meeting check-in with every team member present. Therefore, the ICM team leader must develop an efficient, effective communication system for the team—a communication system based on the belief that you can trust your fellow team members to cover for you, and you can call them as often as needed on any given day.

The team leader leads by setting an example that team members want to emulate. In all facets of the position, the team leader always sets the tone and creates an environment in which the entire team can practice strengths-based, recovery-focused case management. Whether acting as a clinical supervisor, a mentor, or a service provider, the team leader is always a good problem solver, is always committed to professionalism, is always able to work in a team environment, and is always willing to learn new things. An effective team leader must also be creative, intelligent, organized, ethical, and able to manage stress well by practicing self-care. Since every day holds new challenges and crises, the team leader must be able to think quickly to manage all situations.

Intensive Case Managers

Intensive case managers must bring to their work the recovery-focused values and principles that are consistent with the PHF program. To better understand the larger context of their client's conditions, intensive case managers ideally have a social justice perspective—or perhaps it is more accurate to say a "social injustice awareness" of some of the root causes of homelessness. To be productive and effective as clinicians, intensive case managers must be very good listeners, empathic, and comfortable with encouraging and supporting their clients as they work to improve their lives.

PHF intensive case managers must also be resourceful and have good research and advocacy skills. First and foremost, they need to be able to find all the resources needed by their clients and then ensure that clients can have easy access to these services. Since case managers often work independently, they must be ethical, motivated, capable of setting priorities, and able to flexibly juggle many tasks at the same time.

Intensive case managers need to understand that the focus of treatment is not on "fixing" a client, but on building a client's core competencies. In the words of Dr. Charles Rapp in *Case Management for Mentally Ill Patients: Theory and Practice* (Harris and Bergman, 1993), "People tend to develop and grow based on individual interests, aspirations, and strengths. We like to spend time doing things we do well and that have meaning to us."[22] Effective case managers understand that they must form a creative problem-solving partnership with each and every client.

Generally speaking, in the PHF context, ICM case managers hold at least one master's degree in psychology, social work, or another related field.

A *day in the life of a PHF intensive case manager*

Sarah Knight, intensive case manager at Pathways to Housing DC, describes three of her typical days on the job in her following diary excerpts. Her accounts demonstrate the far-reaching and varied aspects of this PHF role and poignantly reveal the unique relationship between PHF clients and teams.

Daily Log, April 6–8, 2010
Sarah Knight, Intensive Case Manager
Pathways to Housing DC

Tuesday, April 6

7:00 a.m. I arrived at the office to gather documents, paperwork, and other necessary items before leaving in a company vehicle at 7:30.

8:00 I arrived at the home of the first client. After checking that he was prepared with his ID, insurance card, and list of current meds, I accompanied him to his physical. His last physical was at least three years ago. En route to the clinic, he spoke about his brother's latest health diagnosis; his brother's cancer had advanced. I discussed the importance of sufficient social support networks in difficult times. His appointment went smoothly, and he scheduled a follow-up appointment in two weeks and made an appointment to see the clinic's podiatrist. Then I assisted him in adding minutes to his cell phone and in obtaining money orders to pay his monthly rent portion and utility bills. I also assisted him in bringing his rent portion to his landlord. We then set a time to meet in the office to review his Treatment Plan.

While he was in the exam room, I made a variety of phone calls, including a call to a landlord regarding leaving the utility room door unlocked to allow the electric company to perform meter readings, a call to another client to confirm his psychiatrist appointment and home visit appointment later in the week, and I made several unanswered phone calls to a client who had been unavailable during the previous week.

12:00 I took a lunch break at the office and began to enter case notes.

12:45 p.m. I met with second client at the shelter where she is living. I brought her the over-the-counter indigestion medicine she requested. I described an apartment I would be viewing on her behalf the following day. We discussed her opinion about the location, unit, and I told her about other possible units in different areas of the city. She adamantly expressed her discomfort with most areas of the city; she cited past experiences of witnessing street violence. I acknowledged her desire to live in a safe location, but did state that since the city has changed drastically in the past several years, certain neighborhoods are now safer than they were previously. I encouraged her to speak to friends and shelter staff about various DC neighborhoods in hopes that her comfort zone would widen, increasing her options. We set a time for our next meeting. She stated that she had no other immediate needs. She said her medication is working effectively and that she will not need a follow-up appointment with the podiatrist for at least another month.

1:40 I returned to the office for Wellness Self-Management Group at 2 p.m. One group participant arrived early to discuss a personal issue. She explained that she feels that her partner expects her to provide unreasonable amounts of financial assistance. She stated that she struggles with wanting to be supportive but also wants to save money for her future goal of moving. She said she often ends up feeling guilty or being yelled at by her partner when the topic of money is broached. We discussed the importance of engaging in positive and balanced relationships in which the needs and goals of each party are respected. We engaged in a mock discussion in which she practiced verbalizing her concerns and feelings. We discussed how and when she might initiate a similar conversation with her partner. We then set a date to do shopping for household cleaning goods. She related that she plans to take the final part of the GED practice exam the coming week at the local public library, and she plans to take the GED exam within the month.

2:00   I facilitated a session of the weekly Wellness Self-Management Group. The meeting was an introductory session for a new group. Curriculum content, goals of the program, and personal expectations were discussed.

3:00   Following group, I met briefly with another group participant to help her complete an energy assistance application. We discussed her medical appointment schedule for the remainder of the week and confirmed time and date of her intake appointment at a local food assistance agency.

3:20   I met with team leader for weekly supervision. We discussed my caseload and status of each consumer and developed strategies for engaging several clients who were becoming increasingly withdrawn.

4:00   I arrived at the residence of a client whom I had been unable to contact by house phone or cell phone for several days. His cell phone seemed to be disconnected, which was uncharacteristic of him. I used the agency's copy of his apartment key to enter the unit when my knocks were unanswered. The client was not in his residence. I left my card and a request for him to call me.

4:30–5:00   I entered case notes from my home computer.

Wednesday, April 7

7:30 a.m.   I arrived at the office to get items needed for the day and to pick up a company vehicle.

8:00   Met with first client of the day at her apartment. I assisted her in obtaining a money order to mail to the electric company. She has been very worried about finances recently. Through a miscommunication between Social Security and DC Medicaid, her disability income was temporarily reduced. She will be reimbursed for the difference, but the setback has been a big source of anxiety for her. We discussed the many helpful community resources that she can access this month to ensure that she is not lacking in food or other necessities. She had received a notice from her building's management regarding an extermination set to take place that day. She was anxious that her apartment was too cluttered and that it was not ready to be seen by anyone associated with building management. I assisted her in calling the management office for a better description of how to ready an apartment for extermination. She became slightly more relaxed after hearing the steps she needed to take to prep her apartment. She stated that she felt prepared for the exterminators to come. She told me that her sister had called the previous night and sent me her best wishes. She became emotional as she thanked me for being there for her.

8:50 I picked up another client at her apartment and accompanied her to a local food bank for intake. It has been difficult for her to accept that she needs to access community resources that give food assistance. She still declines to apply for food stamps; she states that others need the help more than she does. Due to recent increases in her medical expenses, she has decided to become connected with at least one food bank resource. The intake worker at the food bank encouraged her to apply for food stamps and provided her with further information about other community resources. After leaving the food bank, I assisted the client, who has very limited mobility, in shopping for household cleaning supplies. We discussed her upcoming appointment at DC Housing Authority.

11:15 I arrived at a client's apartment for our appointment to run errands. About twenty-five minutes after I arrived, he was ready to leave his apartment. I accompanied him as he added minutes to his cell phone, purchased new rubber tips for his cane, and purchased household cleaning supplies. At his apartment, we completed his monthly Home Visit Report. He identified the broken toilet seat as the only needed repair. We discussed his budgeting skills. The client has a tendency to spend his money within the first week of the month, leaving him without anything for the remaining weeks. He stated that he is doing better this month and has some money remaining. We discussed a plan for establishing a weekly spending goal and then tracking actual expenditures to see how reality matches with the projected goal. We specifically discussed noting how much money he spends on alcohol and talked about alternate uses for this money. He also updated me on his paper sales from the previous week. He is a Street Sense vendor and takes pride in the work that he does. He is also a DC native and always makes a point to share stories of the buildings and places that we pass as we drive through the city together.

1:00 p.m. I returned to the office to drop off the car for a teammate to use. I ate a quick lunch and made phone calls to determine a client's payment options for overdue electric bills.

I made more calls to local hospitals to try to locate a client. Calls were unsuccessful. I called his emergency contact and left a message requesting a return phone call.

I spoke with a client to confirm our appointment for the following morning. The client was intoxicated and very emotional as he informed me that his aunt was put on life support the previous night. He drinks to manage the emotional pain associated with the deaths of his loved ones. He attends funerals almost weekly and collects funeral bulletins. He recently became connected with a psychologist in the community, although his attendance at appointments is still very inconsistent. We discussed what activities he might undertake during the remainder of his day to lift his mood; a nap followed by a walk outside was the course of action on which he settled. The phone call ended with the client's standard parting phrase of "Thank you, I love you. I love you, thank you."

3:15 I arrived at the home of my last appointment for the day. I had called this client earlier in the day to confirm that he was at home (he is very forgetful and is often gone from his apartment from 5 a.m. until 5 p.m.). He answered his phone, became confused about who was calling, hung up, and did not answer the phone again. When I arrived at his apartment, he answered the door in his underwear. I asked him if he would prefer to get dressed before I came in; he fumbled around looking for clothes and settled with sitting under a blanket on his couch. I asked him why he had not been home on Monday to be accompanied to his doctor's appointment, and he stated that he had changed his mind about going to the doctor. He has had concerns that a doctor will sell his blood and/or operate on him if he goes in for a physical. He had decided he was willing to go once as a test run but was unavailable on the morning of the appointment. I reassured him that if he decides he would like to see a doctor, I would be with him during the appointment to ensure that nothing he is uncomfortable with will happen. We then discussed his recent behavior in the building. The previous week, several complaints were made against him for being undressed in the hallway, sleeping in the trash room, and refusing to let maintenance personnel in his unit. Building management stated that he is one incident away from eviction. He explained that he has been sleeping in his apartment and has not had altercations with maintenance personnel or neighbors in the past few days. He was very honest and explained that he is still allowing his friend to stay with him, even though he understands this to be a violation of his lease. He maintains that just as people helped him when he had nothing, it is his duty to help others now that he has so much to offer. We confirmed his appointment to speak with the housing coordinator the following day at 11 a.m. I wrote the time and date on a card and placed it on his fridge in hopes that he would remember to stay at home to be accompanied to the appointment.

4:00 I spent a little time catching up on case notes before calling it a day.

Thursday, April 8

8:00 a.m. I arrived at the office ready to start the day.

9:00 I arrived at my first appointment for the day. The agenda was to do a little shopping, put money on a smart trip card, and provide the client with information about upcoming groups at Pathways. The client drinks heavily, but secretly. He is always very embarrassed when one of our meetings coincides with one of his binges. This morning, he came out of his apartment to go shopping, weaving the whole way to the car. I asked him if he felt well enough to stick with the original plan; he stated that he did. He began almost immediately to talk about his uncle, who had been put on life support the previous night. When I spoke with him the previous day to confirm our appointment, he told me that his aunt had been put on life support. I redirected the client to focus on picking up necessity items only and said we could discuss his feelings when we returned home. During the remainder of the abbreviated shopping trip, he would periodically dissolve into statements of *"why me, why me, why...."* At his apartment, he became very sullen and asked me, "Sister, do you think I'm crazy?" He is very worried about how he appears to others. He takes great pride in his personal appearance and attempts to hide his sexuality and his drinking habits, as he is convinced both make people look down on him. I asked him if we could have a very honest conversation. He said yes. We engaged in a conversation that we have had previously, both when he has been intoxicated and sober.

"Do you feel that the grief you experience, due to loss of loved ones, interferes with your ability to accomplish what you would like to accomplish in your day-to-day life?"

"Yes."

"Do you drink to manage the pain you feel?"

"Yes. I drink to distract myself, or to try and think about other things."

"Does that work?"

"Not at all."

At this point, he began to cry and buried his head in my shoulder. I told him that while the pain he feels is no small thing, he can learn to manage his symptoms of depression and live a life in which his sadness does not prevent him from accomplishing his goals. We discussed maintaining regular appointments with his psychiatrist and being honest with his psychiatrist so he can receive the most accurate help. We discussed participating in positive activities so that he can feel purposeful in his life and can maintain a positive outlook. I then provided the client with the information I had brought about gardening, yoga, and wellness groups. He said he was very interested in all the proposed activities. He asked me if I would ever leave him. I assured the client that I had no plans to leave Pathways soon but did remind him that it was more than likely he would have a different case manager some day. I reminded him that he provides his own motivation to change, and that while I enjoy working with him, he has the insight and strength necessary to accomplish the goals he sets for himself. As our meeting drew to a close, I asked him to name five things for which he is grateful. We discussed focusing on these positive thoughts throughout the day. We discussed activities in which he can engage throughout the day.

10:15 My next appointment was in the next apartment building over with a client who has recently been diagnosed with diabetes. He has been struggling with accepting a new routine of taking medication daily, checking his blood sugar daily, and seeing his doctor regularly. He has been working on keeping a daily journal of his blood sugar scores. He showed me his notebook listing his scores since our last meeting three days earlier. His scores have continued to drop; they have finally reached the top of the healthy range! He keeps his meds in a med container, with one spot for each day. He is becoming more consistent with taking his meds as prescribed. We discussed how exciting the results of taking meds as prescribed are (healthy blood sugar levels). I also presented him with the option of seeing a Pathways psychiatrist one time for an assessment to determine if he can qualify for more benefits. He does not currently receive any income. He stated he was not interested. He said he had needed to consider seeing a doctor for several months before actually seeing the doctor who gave him his diabetes diagnosis two months ago. Deciding to seek any sort of medical care is a long process for this particular client.

11:15 I arrived at the apartment of the client who had an appointment that afternoon with the housing coordinator to discuss problems he had been having recently in the building, including being undressed in the hallway, sleeping in the trash room, and having conflict with maintenance personnel. He said he was not feeling well that day but stated he did still wish to go to his appointment. During the meeting, I translated for him as the housing coordinator expressed the concerns of the landlord and as he expressed his own perspective on recent events. The client admitted that one particular maintenance man has been making mean comments about him accepting government support and not doing his fair share of work. He said he is very offended by such accusations. He was a participant of the Pathways program for one year, and two blizzards, before he was finally ready to accept housing. Being accused of taking handouts is very hurtful to him. The housing coordinator explained her role in mediating between clients and landlords to ensure that clients can smoothly assume the role of tenant. She explained that all parties (housing coordinator, case manager, landlord, and client) can and should be involved in helping the client in his time of transition. The client expressed satisfaction with the outcome of the meeting. He did, however, continue to maintain that it is his duty to God and men to use his apartment to help others by providing them with temporary shelter. Before taking him home, we picked up some antinausea, antidiarrhea medicine and some groceries from the store. We discussed the course of action to take if he develops a fever or if his condition gets much worse. We also discussed going to the doctor as a walk-in on the coming Monday.

During the drive to and from the housing coordinator's office, the client shared with me memories of spending Semana Santa at the beach in Guatemala. He is very chatty and loves to share stories from past experiences. His stories often take outlandish turns, but regardless of base in reality, the conversation is always very pleasant.

2:45 p.m. I arrived at the apartment of another client who had recently switched her benefits from MD to DC. April was the first month in which she was receiving food stamps from DC. Her EBT card, however, was not functioning properly. I assisted her in contacting the EBT training center and an IMA representative to rectify the problem. Her account had a block placed on it, but we were assured that the block would be removed and her card would be functioning the following day.

3:45 I arrived for my last appointment of the day. This client has been grieving the loss of his wife, who passed away less than two weeks after they move into their apartment. He has also made several visits to the ER since her passing to have the parasites in his skull examined. He states that the parasites are causing myriad other body aches and pains. He has also become increasingly isolated to avoid spreading this parasite to others. He went into a long description of their recent activity and showed me the fibers that they expel that he collects. He stated that he has been using the prescription shampoos and lotions his doctor prescribed him; he is not convinced they are helping. He also stated that he believes a cat or other animal is living in his apartment wall. We discussed having an exterminator come into his apartment to address the problem and discussed the outcome of his psych appt. the previous day. I reminded him that further services, such as group grief counseling, can be available to him if he chooses to access them. He stated that he will likely go to his parents in Maryland for the weekend to visit his son. We also discussed a plan to go the Social Security office and to do laundry the following week.

5:15 I dropped the car back at the office and ended another day of work.

The Program Assistant

Responsibilities of the PHF ICM team's program assistant are similar to those of the ACT team's program assistant, described previously: he or she helps with meeting logistics, updates charts, and generally keeps the ICM team's paperwork organized. The program assistant is frequently the first person to greet clients when they come to the office and is therefore responsible for creating a welcoming and safe environment. He or she also handles petty cash disbursements and other program supplies and supports the team in a number of ways.

The ICM Weekly Team Meeting

PHF ICM teams meet on a weekly basis (with all team members present), to discuss clients with whom they are working and to report any significant changes in services. This is an opportune time for team members to share information so they all have a basic understanding of each client's strengths, desires, and goals. Team members will brief the next person who will start the on-call rotation about any clients who are having difficulties and any crisis plans that may be in place.

The weekly meeting usually takes between two and four hours, depending on the number of clients the team is serving. Teams may meet more frequently if the team leader finds it necessary.

In addition to weekly team meetings, PHF ICM teams meet once a month for case conferences with other relevant partners in outside agencies and with other PHF ICM team members. Clients' strengths and goals are discussed in greater detail at this meeting, and service plans and decisions are made at this time with all providers in the client's life present.

Chapter 6 Summary

The PHF **intensive case management (ICM) team** takes a coordinated and brokered approach that delivers services based on the **strengths model of services**. This model employs six principles outlined by Dr. Charles Rapp in *The Strengths Model,* coauthored with Richard Goscha.

1. People with psychiatric disabilities can recover, reclaim, and transform their lives.

2. It is important to focus on an individual's strengths.

3. The community is viewed as an oasis of resources, not as a barrier.

4. The client is the director of the helping process.

5. The case manager–client relationship is primary and essential.

6. The primary setting for the work is in the community.

Clients continue to receive services even if they lose housing due to eviction, short-term inpatient treatment, or other institutional stays. ICM teams are staffed by a team leader, intensive case managers, and a program assistant; they meet weekly and also hold monthly case conference meetings.

Chapter 7

Incorporating Other Evidence-Based Practices

THIS CHAPTER BRIEFLY DESCRIBES a number of evidence-based practices and clinical interventions that can be very effective with clients served by Pathways Housing First programs. Because these clients often have multiple diagnoses, complex life stories, and long histories of failed treatment, staff working with this population must have excellent clinical skills. The practices described in this chapter are best applied when staff already have the core competencies required of skilled clinicians. They are additions to—not substitutes for—comprehensive clinical training. Of course, PHF clinicians serving on assertive community treatment (ACT) or intensive case management (ICM) teams are not expected to be experts on *all* of the practices described here. One team member may be identified as the team's specialist on substance abuse, another as the wellness specialist, and a third as the Supported Employment (SE) specialist. Team members share their expertise with each other and thus improve the team's overall clinical competence.

Three wide-ranging practices are recommended for PHF programs:

- Integrated dual disorders treatment (IDDT), with the core elements of harm reduction, Stages of Change, and Motivational Interviewing

- Wellness Management and Recovery, including the Wellness Recovery Action Plan (WRAP)

- Supported Employment, which includes Individual Placement and Support

All three are based on the same client-driven and humanistic values and principles that are integral to the PHF program. In the Pathways Housing First context, the ACT and ICM teams' focus on recovery and client self-determination make these evidence-based practices especially compatible with other PHF program practices, and they can easily be incorporated into these teams' clinical work.

 Generally, it is best to introduce a new evidence-based practice into a PHF program after the team has been in operation for a few months and has learned to coordinate the day-to-day activities of obtaining housing and providing clients with clinical and support services. All of these practices are well documented in the mental health field, and practitioners have developed user-friendly "toolkits" for most of them; these kits can be found on the SAMHSA Web site under "Evidence-Based Practices."[23] Again, no single team member is expected to master all of these practices, but the team's collective expertise should include some knowledge of all of them.

The final section of the chapter focuses on Community Integration. One of the ultimate aims of recovery is to help clients integrate into their communities, living independently or with the supports they need.

Integrated Dual Disorders Treatment

The importance of focusing on dual disorders emerged from the facts that substance use disorders are common in people with severe mental illness, and mental illness is common among people with substance use disorders. Unless treated in an integrated manner, these so-called "dual disorders" have poor prognosis and treatment outcomes. This cohort has high rates of hospitalization, financial problems, family problems, interpersonal conflicts, incarceration, morbidity rates for medical problems (including HIV and hepatitis), and early mortality. Traditional treatment treats each condition separately, but separate treatment is not effective.

Given that most PHF clients have a dual diagnosis of mental illness and substance abuse, integrated dual disorders treatment (IDDT) is the most effective approach for addressing these problems. IDDT helps clients identify the magnitude of their addiction and make necessary connections so they can begin to see how their abuse of alcohol and other drugs interferes with their life goals. As described below, the principles of IDDT call for ACT and ICM teams in the PHF program to incorporate a harm-reduction approach when working with clients to address their addictions. IDDT provides a framework to match treatment interventions to a client's process of progressive change.

To successfully implement IDDT, the substance abuse specialist and the entire team must understand the interaction between mental illness and addictions. IDDT incorporates several other SAMHSA-endorsed evidence-based practices, including Motivational Interviewing (MI) and cognitive behavioral therapy (CBT).

PHF clients are often actively using alcohol or other drugs when they enter the program, and they are usually ambivalent about stopping their substance use. That use most often occurs in a social context, so the challenge to give up alcohol and other drugs also involves giving up old friends and acquaintances. It is not simply a question of eliminating a drug or intoxicating substance; it often means giving up a long-held lifestyle that is familiar—albeit self-destructive—in order to adopt a new lifestyle that may hold healthy possibilities but is unfamiliar and yet to be defined.

To effectively discuss and start to resolve clients' natural ambivalence about such large-scale personal change, PHF staff must be highly skilled in the practice of Motivational Interviewing (MI). Staff must also learn about the Stages of Change, a framework for understanding clients' relationships to their addictions. This framework spans several attitudinal stages, from pre-contemplation (denial) to maintenance (sustaining controlled use or sobriety).

Cognitive behavioral therapy (CBT) is very effective in helping clients develop rational ways to identify people or situations that are likely to trigger their alcohol and other drug use, and it teaches clients strategies to cope with these situations and their cravings. CBT also teaches clients a variety of social skills, such as effective strategies for refusing alcohol or other drugs in social situations where clients experience a great deal of peer pressure to use. Clients are also taught to manage the stress that results from these situations. As PHF clinical team members learn MI and CBT in the context of addiction treatment, they start to see how relevant these core clinical competencies are to other areas of clients' lives.

In fact, the PHF clinical teams' approach already has several elements in common with IDDT. Services are longitudinal and client-centered, clients are not required to attain abstinence, and both approaches emphasize building trust and nurturing relationships with clients. Another shared assumption is that psychiatric disability and addiction disorders are often long-standing conditions; both approaches accept the reality that change takes time. Research studies suggest that 60 percent of the clients who receive IDDT will be in remission within four years—*if* the treatment provider maintains a high degree of fidelity to the IDDT model. The PHF and IDDT approaches share a philosophy of working collaboratively with each client and recognizing that progress is not linear. The clinical skills embedded in IDDT help the PHF teams work with clients in a manner that is consistent with clients' own needs.

Basic Implementation Principles of IDDT

When IDDT is effective, it leads not only to reduction or abstinence in substance use, but also to improvements in other areas of clients' lives, including reduced hospitalizations, symptom reduction, reduced violence, reduced victimization and involvement with criminal justice, better physical health, and gains in productive functioning, including employment and improved relationships and family life.

As practiced in the PHF model, the basic implementation principles of IDDT include

- Integrated treatment: Mental health and substance abuse are both viewed as primary diagnoses and are targeted for concurrent treatment.

- Assertive engagement: Staff make every effort to actively engage reluctant clients and to reach out and provide services in the client's natural living environment. They also provide all manner of assistance (both clinical and practical) as a means to develop trust and a working alliance.

• Comprehensive services: PHF clinical teams should offer clients additional interventions such as Supported Employment and Illness Management and Recovery, as well as social skills training and pharmacological treatment.

• Motivation-based treatment: Interventions must be adapted to meet a client's motivation for change, or stage of change. The program's stages of treatment approach provides a framework for assessing the client's motivational state and setting goals, which helps teams and clients select interventions that are appropriate to achieving those goals.

• Harm-reduction approach: The program's focus is to reduce negative consequences of mental illness and substance abuse. The goal here is to try to protect the client from the dire consequences of substance abuse, including a return to homelessness, infectious disease, or incarceration. Developing a good working alliance is key; this includes establishing the ground rules that allow open and honest discussion about the client's drug use without the client fearing negative consequences from that honest discussion.

• Time-unlimited services: IDDT programs do not produce dramatic results over short periods of time. Severe psychiatric disability and addiction are seldom a quick fix. Clients improve gradually, and the program recognizes that individuals recover at their own pace and need to be given enough time and support to achieve this goal.

• Multiple psychotherapeutic modalities: Individual modalities include Motivational Interviewing and cognitive behavioral therapy; group modalities include Stages of Change groups, harm-reduction groups, and self-help groups such as Alcoholics Anonymous, Narcotics Anonymous, and Double Trouble in Recovery, a Twelve Step group specifically for those with multiple disorders. When possible, a family systems or family psycho-education intervention may also be used.

Harm Reduction

As noted earlier, harm reduction is a central component of PHF program. The harm-reduction approach to mental health and addiction treatment includes a set of practical strategies to reduce the negative consequences of harmful behaviors associated with substance abuse. It does not require complete abstinence as a goal of treatment. In the PHF program, harm reduction also includes minimizing the risky behaviors or negative consequences for clients with active psychiatric symptoms who refuse to take medication. It is an essential program component because clients are not required to take medication or attain sobriety as a precondition for housing. Harm reduction is a compassionate and pragmatic alternative to traditional treatment for people who are unwilling or unable to work with the abstinence-based approach. *The goal in harm reduction is to help the client live a better life.*

Harm reduction is solution-focused, compassionate, and pragmatic. This approach simply accepts that some clients will use drugs and refuse medication. It accepts the clients' position on these matters and works with them from where they are to reduce the risks associated with these choices. For example, a PHF team may work with the client who refuses to take medication because voices he hears tell him it "kills his soul." Team members might help him learn ways to lower his own voice when responding to the voices he hears, to avoid disturbing his neighbors who in turn might call the police.

Harm reduction is about observing and celebrating small positive steps. This approach acknowledges any steps in the direction of healthy behaviors or reducing risk. It is about celebrating when a client tells a team member, "I went from drinking a six-pack of beer a day to a forty-ouncer." When the client who has been sober for five weeks tells the harm-reduction group on Monday morning that he relapsed over the weekend, harm reduction is about congratulating him for having fallen off the wagon for only two days and being right back on it on Monday.

Harm reduction requires an individualized approach. A flexible approach must be taken with each client, because clients vary widely with regard to the severity of their addiction or symptoms, their willingness to try different interventions (such as moderation, safer use, or trial abstinence), their psychiatric status, and their personal beliefs, values, strengths, and weaknesses.

PHF programs practice the following principles of harm reduction, which are based on the work of Andrew Tatarsky and G. Alan Marlatt:[24]

- Substance abuse and psychiatric symptoms are best understood and addressed in the context of the whole person in his or her social and cultural environment.

- The relationship between helper and client is one of respect rather than authoritarianism. This is a collaborative relationship in which goals and strategies are discussed and planned jointly.

- The emphasis is on personal choice and responsibility for deciding future behavior.

- Goals are client *directed*. The client's motivation, goals, and strengths determine the course of treatment. The treatment begins with where the client is—psychologically, socially, spiritually, culturally, and even geographically (e.g., home visits). Abstinence (or any other preconceived goal) is not held out as a starting point in treatment.

- Alcohol and other drug use are viewed on a wide continuum of risk from not very risky to life threatening, and the treatment approach matches the severity.

- Engagement in treatment is the primary goal. However, staff members do not insist on change and do not challenge a client's point of view; they must communicate with empathy and that they "get it" and consider that the client has valid reasons to use alcohol or other drugs or to refuse to take medication. (Many clients use alcohol or other drugs to cope with internal or external difficulties.)

- The client's ambivalence about sobriety is honored and made a conscious part of the conversation. Teams use "decisional balance," in which clients are urged to consider the pros and cons of using and not using and to explore reasons to change *and* reasons not to change.

In the PHF context, providing clients who are homeless and dually diagnosed with a safe and secure place to live, regardless of their substance use or psychiatric symptoms, goes a long way toward reducing the harm and risk associated with self-destructive behaviors. Harm reduction is a very effective PHF engagement tool and a way to quickly gain the client's trust.

To reduce harmful behaviors, PHF teams must get to know their clients and familiarize themselves with their clients' patterns of use. Does the client use marijuana and alcohol? Does the client use more when he or she is with former friends from the streets? Is the client able to moderate his or her use if alone in the apartment? Could the client make use of a needle exchange program? Could he or she try to reduce alcohol use, for example, drinking three days a week instead of five? Is the client willing to try "trial abstinence" or take a break from alcohol or other drug use? Does the client need help from the team to manage money for groceries and other basic needs? Many harm-reduction strategies are possible, and the appropriate one will depend on factors that include the client's goals, strengths, and stages of change.

Stages of Change

The Stages of Change model, developed by James Prochaska and Carlo DiClemente, is based on the theory that people alter their behaviors in progressive steps, at their own pace. Prochaska and DiClemente identified five Stages of Change. Relapse—a common occurrence for many clients who struggle with addiction—is included in the maintenance stage. As mentioned in the IDDT discussion earlier, effective treatment means that the stage of treatment must mirror the client's stage of change.

Stage One: Pre-contemplation—At this stage, clients do not believe their substance abuse or behavior is a problem, and they are unable to acknowledge any negative or adverse effects from such behavior. Essentially, the client is in denial. Common traits of Stage One are defensiveness, resistance to suggestions about substance use, and the feeling of being coerced or being controlled.

Stage Two: Contemplation—At this stage, clients are aware that their behavior can result (or has resulted) in harmful consequences. And, during periods when they are not using, they can begin to consider the possibility of a different way to manage their addictions. Clients in Stage Two may voice awareness of the problem yet still believe its significance is low, that they can manage it and "keep it small." While clients may seem to be in the contemplation stage, they may functionally still be in the pre-contemplation stage. Common traits of Stage Two are distress, seeking to evaluate, and a desire for control or mastery.

Stage Three: Preparation—At this point, clients are aware that their substance abuse has negative consequences on their lives. In many cases, clients have learned from successful past attempts to change, and they are starting to figure out how to put those lessons in place. Common traits of Stage Three are intent to change, readiness to change based on action and attitude, and engagement in change process.

Stage Four: Action—At this stage, clients are modifying their behavior or their environment. Common traits of Stage Four are verbalizing a desire to make a change, taking suggestions that help move away from people who are using, and developing friendships with people who are sober, or at least who support their recovery. When they feel like using, they cope by calling on the team, a peer, or a sponsor and asking for assistance.

Stage Five: Maintenance—At this point, clients are sustaining and further incorporating the changes they have already made. They are also actively avoiding relapse. Common traits are discussing what they are doing to maintain these changes, describing situations that are difficult for them (and stating how they cope with them), and talking about how they can avoid relapse.

In the Stages of Change and harm-reduction approach, when relapse happens, it does not mean that all that has been gained is now lost. The key to handling relapse is to intervene immediately and learn from what happened. Relapse is not a result of a character flaw or loss of morality; it is often simply a part of the recovery process. Some signs of impending relapse may include arguing, forgetfulness, stress symptoms, lack of self-care, or moodiness.

Motivational Interviewing

A core clinical skill, Motivational Interviewing (MI) should be part of the basic training curriculum for all staff working in PHF programs—or in any program with a client-driven approach to services. This skill is used in the practices of IDDT, harm reduction, and Wellness Management and Recovery.

MI is a client-directed counseling approach developed by clinical psychologists William R. Miller, Ph.D., and Stephen Rollnick, Ph.D. Its overarching concept is that change is possible and that the desire for change must come from the individual. PHF teams can increase this motivation in a variety of ways, but the client is ultimately responsible for, and in control of, making the change.

The five MI principles, as described by Miller and Rollnick, are listed here:

1. **Avoid argumentation and direct confrontation:** Arguing with and confronting clients can cause them to feel attacked and coerced, which affects their desire to fully participate in treatment. One tenet of MI is that the counselor or team member is present as a facilitator of change, but the client must ultimately drive the change.

2. **Express accurate and genuine empathy:** This involves understanding the client and being able to imagine what it must be like to experience what the client is experiencing. MI uses much of Carl Rogers' work to inform its practice. Rogers used the term "unconditional positive regard" to describe what a client needs to experience to feel comfortable trusting and examining the toll that some behaviors are taking on his or her life.

3. **Support self-efficacy and optimism:** The client and the team members must believe that change is possible. A group setting in which others have had success can be an extremely powerful tool. Building on a client's past success is also a good way to prove that change is possible and that it can be done.

4. **Roll with resistance:** A team member runs the risk of increasing resistance by pushing back and getting into a power struggle with a client. Instead, the team member needs to be flexible and use the client's "momentum" to further explore his or her views.

5. **Heighten discrepancy (use decisional balance):** The team member needs to become adept at helping the client see how his or her behavior is leading him or her either toward or away from current goals.

Numerous techniques have been derived from MI principles and applied to the various Stages of Change. (Remember, PHF teams must match the stage of treatment with the stage of change.) Table 3 illustrates some of these linkages and techniques.

Table 3

Techniques Derived from Stages of Change and Motivational Interviewing

Stage of Change	Motivational Interviewing Principle	Clinical Technique
Pre-contemplation	• Show empathy • Heighten discrepancy ("decisional balance") • Roll with resistance • Avoid argumentation	• Develop rapport • Do not confront • Do elicit discrepancy (client describes how choices either support or undermine goals) • Explore pros and cons of substance abuse • Raise doubts, reframe the issue, take a questioning stance
Contemplation	• Enhance client's self-efficacy • Examine client's value in relation to change • Show empathy	• Elicit positive statements for change; tip the balance toward change • Examine pros and cons of not changing; emphasize the pros • Support positive change; listen to the "talk" the client uses • Reframe and shift focus, take a questioning stance, offer information
Preparation	• Support self-efficacy • Show empathy	• Help client clarify goals, consider and lower barriers to change, explore expectations of change • Assist with learning decisional balance tools; help client elicit social support, ask open-ended questions, listen reflectively • Affirm, educate, offer options of tapering down, consider a trial of moderation
Action	• Show empathy • Avoid doing for; do with • Support self-efficacy	• Affirm and help develop plans for realistic change • Educate, help create and strengthen a support network, improve problem-solving skills, anticipate problems, tolerate affect and the fear of ambivalence • Strengthen and support the client's commitment for change
Maintenance	• Support self-efficacy • Show empathy	• Broaden community support • Affirm the client; review long-term goals and relapse prevention plans

When a client relapses, the PHF clinical team needs to maintain empathy and help the client examine what happened to learn from the experience and build on what has already been gained. The client may seem to have returned to an earlier stage of change; the team must work with the client there, encouraging the client to see this as an opportunity to learn in order to avoid future relapses.

Wellness Management and Recovery

One of the most important goals of a PHF program is to facilitate a client's wellness and recovery. This goal guides all of the program's clinical teams' actions as an integral part of daily practice. This approach is also known as Illness Management and Recovery, or IMR. As with the other evidence-based practices, this is not just the job of the wellness specialist; it is the job of everyone on the team. The specialist's job is to help the team remain focused on wellness, provide any new information related to wellness, and link relevant treatment interventions to this overarching goal.

The first rule of wellness management is to treat clients with respect at all times. Again, the values and principles of these evidence-based practices are consistent with PHF principles. Treating clients in a nonjudgmental manner and allowing them to make their own decisions—even when the team disagrees—is key to building a strong therapeutic alliance.

For wellness and recovery to occur, there needs to be a *fundamental shift in power from the clinician as expert to the client as expert.* Decisions about treatment are ultimately made by the client. PHF clinical teams need to be very conscious and deliberate and prevent any form of coercion—both explicit and implicit—in their day-to-day interactions with clients, especially during treatment sessions.

Using "person first" language in discussions with and about clients conveys the necessary respect and empathy to establish positive collaborative relationships. Team members learn never to refer to clients by their diagnosis, always to speak about the client as though he or she were in the room, and not to plan anything for the client unless he or she approves the plan. One well-known phrase from the consumer movement that captures some of these sentiments is "nothing about us without us!"

The principles of a Wellness Management and Recovery approach are consistent with many others in the PHF program, including these:

- **Hopefulness:** The team promotes the shared belief among all involved that change and recovery are possible and that the client can achieve a better quality of life.

- **Empowerment:** The team encourages clients to be as independent as possible.

- **Shared decision making:** Team and clients collaborate on all decisions. Clients set their own agendas and are considered the experts on their illnesses.

- **Developing natural supports:** The team helps clients develop community supports (beyond mental health supports).

- **Assuming normalized roles:** The team helps clients reintegrate into the community and assume normalized roles, such as employee, student, neighbor, tenant, mother, brother, sister, boyfriend, girlfriend, parent, citizen, and so on.

- **Education:** The team provides information on various treatment modalities so clients can make informed decisions about what services they feel would be beneficial.

PHF interventions need to address the psychological, physical, practical, economic, and spiritual needs of the clients they serve. Physical health, exercise, proper nutrition, and attention to health care are as important as adherence to psychiatric medications. This requires training and education in Wellness Management and Recovery for both PHF staff and clients. Curricula and manuals are available at the SAMHSA Web site (see the IMR toolkit) and from the New York State Office of Mental Health: Wellness Self Management Initiative. These materials can provide PHF staff with a script and a roadmap to work with clients in the area of wellness and recovery.

Working on wellness and recovery also provides clients with a greater sense of control and security about what is manageable in their own lives. Clients can choose just how much they wish to disclose in these sessions. They help both parties stay on track.

In addition to the materials mentioned earlier, some other commonly used curricula include these:

- **The Wellness Recovery Action Plan:** Mary Ellen Copeland developed the WRAP in 1997 and tailored it to clients' particular circumstances and needs. Like other effective approaches, it is highly individualized. Clients use a "wellness toolbox" of strategies and information, including daily activities and routines to maintain wellness, to identify the early warning signs of becoming symptomatic, and to reduce the prominence or exacerbation of symptoms.

- **The WRAP toolbox:** This includes a crisis plan when more extraordinary steps may be necessary—including hospitalization. A client's WRAP can be developed in one full-day session or in anywhere from four to ten sessions, in a group or one-to-one setting. Clients are supported in developing the plan, including how they want to be treated and by whom they want to be treated—especially if they are experiencing psychotic or delusional symptoms and cannot make the decision at the time. In this way, the crisis plan is a specific application of an Advance Directive. The crisis plan should be very specific, including where the client would want to be taken (hospital or crisis center?), who should accompany them, how they want to be treated (left alone in a quiet place or have someone to stay with them?), what to drink and eat, and so on. It is very useful for PHF programs to develop a WRAP for every client they serve.

- **Illness Management and Recovery:** Kim Mueser and Susan Gingrich developed the IMR approach at Dartmouth in 2002. (Their expanded and updated IMR curriculum will be available in spring 2011 under the Dartmouth PRC–Hazelden imprint.) Also referred to as Wellness Management and Recovery, this approach has been designated an evidence-based practice. The curriculum consists of eleven modules covering a variety of topics important to wellness and recovery. It can be conducted in a group or in a one-to-one setting, with sessions ranging from fifteen minutes to one hour. IMR takes from nine to twelve months to complete. Research shows that this curriculum can result in better illness management, symptom reduction, and improvements in a variety of psychosocial areas of functioning.

- **Road to Recovery:** Developed by Magellan Behavioral Healthcare and Lori Ashcroft from *Innovations in Recovery* in 2008, *Road to Recovery* is an interactive online teaching curriculum that works in a group or one-to-one setting. It consists of ten lessons on recovery and resilience, supplementing each topic with client videos.

Supported Employment

> *Nothing that I have studied has the same kind of impact on people that employment does.*
>
> **Dr. Robert Drake, Dartmouth Psychiatric Research Center**

As described in chapter 5, the PHF team includes a Supported Employment (SE) specialist who uses an "individual placement and support" approach. If clients express an interest in working, the SE specialist assists them in seeking, gaining, and keeping employment as soon as possible. The SE specialist explores the client's career or vocational interests and helps the client find the position best suited to his or her preferences.

Though the SE specialist is the point person for employment, it must be a team effort. Work is not just the specialist's business; work is everybody's business. This adage is particularly relevant to employment because the team needs every member's support to develop a network of potential job opportunities. Personal and professional connections are very important ways to build these networks. Once a client is employed, staff must provide both the practical and emotional support needed for the client to succeed. Support may be offered at the job site or off-site. Among the techniques and skills required for effective employment placements are job coaching, teaching the necessary job skills, and providing counseling and other ongoing support targeted toward workplace success.

The entire PHF program follows these principles of Supported Employment:

- **Zero exclusion:** No client who expresses an interest in working should be dismissed.

- **Benefits counseling:** Provide clients with clear, accurate, and easy-to-understand information about the impact of employment on entitlements.

- **Rapid job search:** Start the process immediately and try to secure employment for a client in about six months.

- **Competitive employment as the goal:** The goal is to find clients paying jobs in the marketplace. Education and volunteer work are not as highly regarded by SE theory, but in PHF programs, if going to school or volunteering is the client's first choice, client choice trumps theory.

- **Client preference:** The client directs the job search.

- **Follow-along supports can be indefinite:** The team will provide support to the client for as long as the client wants it.

- **Coordinated efforts:** Employment efforts and clinical efforts are closely coordinated.

It is important that the PHF team have frequent discussions about the value of work, and that all team members believe that work is a realistic goal for the clients. It can be helpful to remind the team to apply the Stages of Change model to determine the client's own beliefs and attitudes about the possibility for employment.

The team should set goals for the number of clients employed. If, for example, the team has 10 percent of its clients working, the team can set a new goal to increase it to 30 percent the following year.

Many of these ideas are based on the work of Dr. Robert Drake and Deborah Becker.

Groups and Social Events

Every day includes a wide range of activities for the PHF team and the program clients.

A number of groups are formed around common interests, and they are open to all clients. For example, a cooking group can offer a way for clients to gather for an educational and enjoyable experience, and it can be another avenue for client engagement. Diet is an important part of a client's health and well-being. Learning useful shopping or cooking tips, recipes, and nutritional information contributes to health awareness, connection, and self-responsibility. In cooking group, clients participate in preparing a meal with the team nurse or another team member, and then they enjoy the meal that they have created together.

While the clients enjoy their food, it is a good time for the PHF employment specialist to use the group's interest and experience in food preparation to segue into employment ideas. Through both group and one-on-one meetings, clients formulate ideas and take steps to find rewarding employment, again motivated by choice. When clients say they want to find work in a specific field, the team works with the client to achieve that goal.

Employment-related issues that arise for clients are not out of the ordinary. Like most people, clients who are working, taking classes, attending treatment groups, and perhaps helping to take care of a new child in their life can be overwhelmed. Because the ACT and ICM teams *are* teams in the PHF setting, all members share information and ideas and work together with clients on employment issues— not just the vocational specialist charged with the task. The nurse, team leader, substance abuse specialist, and other team members can all help the client search for a job and also help the client manage his or her time.

PHF clients begin to see themselves as individuals with a future and as individuals in recovery. Their life struggles and creative potentials are honored and celebrated as part of the program. PHF conducts a variety of specialty groups supported by the program, such as arts or photography workshops. These help clients engage in the creative process and share in cultural events, seeing the beauty around them and the fine work they can create. These and other activities operate from a strengths approach, and the PHF program celebrates clients' talents as well as their unique perspectives and experiences. Clients have the opportunity to explore all aspects of their recovery in a wide variety of supportive and inclusive groups.

The program can sponsor and facilitate many groups, including computer classes, a science club, a harm-reduction group, a men's group, a women's group, a monthly tenants' meeting, and others. Staff members also encourage clients to seek out relevant groups and supports in their communities.

Community Integration

In the last few years at Pathways Housing First, there has been a dramatic shift in the work of ACT and ICM teams to provide services and interventions that, instead of fostering dependency on the provider, foster empowerment and self-determination in the client. One way to achieve this broader goal is to help clients develop natural supports in the community. These support networks can include family, friends, neighbors, peers, co-workers, fellow students, or fellow worshipers.

There are a number of ways to facilitate the growth of these natural supports:

1. **Community Resources:** After discussing clients' interests, the PHF team helps clients learn about the resources in their communities. Team members also assess any barriers that may prevent clients from following through in obtaining community support, and they try to develop strategies for clients to use when entering into new situations.

2. **"Circles of support":** In this client group activity, each client takes a turn at the center of a circle of other clients. Each client lists the diverse supports that radiate in and out of the center. It may be time to reconnect clients with relatives—their immediate family or their children or grandchildren. This activity and the discussion surrounding it are a very good way to visually represent family members who are there and who are missing in a client's potential circle of support.

3. **Peer support groups:** A number of peer support groups are available in most communities, including Twelve Step groups such as Alcoholics Anonymous (AA), Narcotics Anonymous (NA), and Emotions Anonymous (EA). There are also groups specifically for clients with co-occurring substance use and mental health disorders,

such as Double Trouble in Recovery (DTR) and Dual Recovery Anonymous (DRA), where, unlike in AA and NA, members are encouraged to talk about multiple disorders.[25]

4. **Activities:** Natural supports can also be addressed through participation in social, recreation, political, and religious activities. The client may meet new people naturally if he or she gets a job, returns to school, attends religious services, or joins an exercise class. Attending activities and social and cultural events, attending sporting events, taking walks in the park, participating in political demonstrations, or volunteering at a favorite nonprofit agency are all community activities that provide opportunities to increase citizenship and meet people with similar beliefs and values.

There are tremendous cultural and ethno-racial variations among all the peoples served by PHF programs. Staff members sometimes have cultural backgrounds similar to their clients', but more important is that each and every staff member recognize, learn about, and honor the cultures of the clients they serve. Community integration and citizenship, as with all of the practices discussed in this chapter, is an individualized process. The optimal fit will be achieved when staff follow the clients' cues and help them find and join the community of their choice.

Chapter 7 Summary

To best serve its clients, the Housing First approach can draw on many other evidence-based practices, including these:

Integrated dual disorders treatment (IDDT) is an evidence-based treatment approach for clients with co-occurring substance disorders and mental illness. IDDT helps clients make connections so they begin to see how their abuse of alcohol and other drugs interferes with their goals. This approach provides a framework to match treatment interventions to a client's openness to progressive change. IDDT incorporates several other SAMHSA-endorsed, evidence-based practices, including Motivational Interviewing (MI), cognitive behavioral therapy (CBT), Wellness Management and Recovery (also called Illness Management and Recovery, or IMR), Supported Employment (SE), and family psycho-education.

The **Stages of Change** model, developed by James Prochaska and Carlo DiClemente, is based on the theory that people change behaviors in progressive steps, at their own pace.

Wellness Management and Recovery (or Illness Management and Recovery—IMR) is a nonjudgmental, "person-first" treatment approach that empowers clients to direct their own recovery.

Supported Employment is a PHF service offered to clients who express an interest in gaining employment. Supported Employment utilizes an Individual Placement and Support (IPS) style and is overseen by a PHF employment specialist.

Community integration is a way to help clients develop natural supports in the community. These support networks can include family, friends, neighbors, peers, co-workers, fellow students, or fellow worshipers.

Chapter 8

Bringing Pathways Housing First to Your Community

THIS CHAPTER OUTLINES THE STEPS AND COMPONENTS needed to bring a Pathways Housing First (PHF) program into your agency or community. It assumes that the entity implementing the program is a not-for-profit entity that will seek government funding for PHF housing and support services. It provides guidance on how to determine the need for a PHF program, discusses how the program may best fit into the context of existing services, and suggests possible sources of funding for the housing and support services components.

Assessing the Need and Making the Case for a PHF Program

The first step to determining whether to implement a PHF program is to evaluate the community's need for such a program. In smaller cities, this evaluation may be done by simply convening a meeting with the local providers. In large cities, the needs assessment data can most likely be found in databases in the social services, mental health, and criminal justice departments.

In all cases, the key questions to be answered at initial meetings or by scrutinizing relevant data are these:

- Are there people in your community who are experiencing homelessness as well as psychiatric disabilities and co-occurring disorders, and who remain chronically homeless even after receiving all available services?

- Are there people known to the shelters, emergency rooms, and police who are frequent users of their services who remain homeless?

If the answer to these questions is yes, there is need for a PHF program because it can effectively house and treat these clients.

Today, hundreds of communities across the United States, Canada, and Europe have determined that there is a need for a PHF program. As mentioned in chapter 1, in the United States where data on the planning process is available, the National Alliance to End Homelessness lists local ten-year plans to end homelessness on its Web site. Of the more than 400 plans listed, about 70 percent include a Housing First program component. The Mental Health Commission of Canada recently invested $110 million to end chronic homelessness for people with mental health problems, introducing PHF programs in five Canadian cities (www.mental healthcommission.ca). A similar national PHF initiative is underway in France, and in Portugal one PHF team has been implemented, with plans for others in the near future.

It is clear that the need for PHF programs is great, and that people with momentum and enthusiasm are bringing them to many cities. However, a great many steps must be taken between identifying the need and gathering together the people and resources needed bring a PHF program to life.

A Local Champion: One Key to Successful Implementation

A local champion is the person who initiates the process of change in a community or an agency. He or she engages other key stakeholders, identifies sources of funding, coordinates grant applications, and generally oversees the implementation of a PHF program. This is the person who reaches out and engages the technical assistance needed to begin the program; the person who works closely and collaboratively with all parties to ensure a smooth and efficient implementation.

Throughout PHF's history, we have had the honor to work with many local champions in a variety of settings and jurisdictions. Patty White is one such remarkable person, and her story highlights some of the challenges others may encounter when they seek to implement a PHF program.

As a director of shelter services in Hartford, Connecticut, Patty White noticed a number of shelter guests who were not doing well in her program. Most people came into the shelter for a brief period of time and then found their way back into housing. The group Patty was concerned with used the shelter intermittently for months and years; they had co-occurring disorders and a host of other health and behavior problems. When shelter staff referred them to existing housing providers, they were always refused admission because they were using drugs and alcohol and would not agree to treatment or sobriety before housing. Patty found this intolerable, so she decided to try something new.

After a couple of meetings with Pathways staff, Patty decided she would implement a PHF program to complement the shelter program. She first had to persuade her board of directors to accept this PHF model—a harm-reduction model that in some ways incurred more risk than they were used to taking. Patty obtained a HUD Supportive Housing Program grant and was finally able to refer and accept her most vulnerable clients into her own PHF program.

Patty White succeeded in implementing a PHF program because the necessary elements were in place. These five elements are key to launching a PHF program through an existing agency.

1. The leadership of the agency, the executive director, and the board of directors must support adopting the model.

2. The staff must see the PHF program as a solution for a group of clients who are currently not well served by existing services.

3. Leadership and staff must embrace the core idea of housing offered as a basic right, rather than a privilege that must be earned through demonstrating compliance with treatment or program rules.

4. Leadership and staff must learn and embrace a harm-reduction model in working with co-occurring disorders.

5. Ideally, new funding must be identified to implement the PHF program.

There is always some period of adjustment when a new program model is implemented, especially one that differs in value orientation and practice from existing programs. Once that initial adjustment is made and the PHF program has been operating for a few months, people in the agency or community begin to appreciate that PHF is able to engage and house people who have been homeless for years. Soon, acceptance of PHF among other providers also grows.

Other notable local champions include Nancy Travers, Director of Housing Services (Department of Social Services), who introduced PHF to New York's Westchester County shelter system long before such an idea was popular. In Utah, Lloyd Pendelton brought PHF to the Salt Lake City provider community and then to the surrounding counties throughout the state. John Parvensky, CEO of the Colorado Coalition for the Homeless, introduced the PHF model into his existing programs and then to Denver mayor John Hickenlooper, who embedded the Housing First approach into Denver's program to end homelessness. A similar policy shift took place in Washington, DC, when mayor Adrian Fenty adopted our Pathways to Housing DC program to end homelessness.

At a national level, Philip Mangano, formerly the executive director of the U.S. Interagency Council on Homelessness, and Nan Roman, president and CEO of the National Alliance to End Homelessness, advocated for adopting Housing First both as intervention and strategy. In Canada, when senator Michael Kirby secured a $110 million project for the Mental Health Commission of Canada to end homelessness, Dr. Paula Goering of the University of Toronto selected Housing First as the intervention for the five-city project.

We include these examples to illustrate how the PHF model has been expanded from a program to a strategy. Essentially, adopting a Housing First strategy means that an agency or a group of agencies (such as a coalition of city programs for the homeless) adopt a policy aimed at providing immediate access to permanent housing and reducing or eliminating the transitional housing and other housing-readiness programs in their system.

Obtaining Funding for the Two PHF Program Components

A PHF program requires two funding streams:

1. Rental support to rent available apartments at fair market value

2. Funds for the program's support and clinical services (either ACT or ICM, depending on the population to be served)

A challenge found at most sites is the fact that the funding for the housing component and for the support services come from different sources. *Regardless of the source of funding, bear in mind that PHF is a permanent supported housing program.* Thus, the funding obtained for a PHF program must be secure for a long period of time because the clients housed by the program will need assistance with paying rent for many years.

How to Pay the Rent

In the United States and Canada, the federal government is the largest source of rental funding. The U.S. Department of Housing and Urban Development (HUD) provides a number of funding options, some of which cover rent only (Section 8); others cover rent and services (Supportive Housing Programs); and still another links HUD rent subsidies to local matching funds for the services (Shelter Plus Care).

One of the nation's best sources of rental funding is the tenant-based housing choice voucher, also known as the Section 8 housing voucher. Clients who qualify for this voucher must be living well below the poverty line. Section 8 funds are adjusted by locality to meet fair-market rent costs, and the tenant must contribute 30 percent of his or her income toward rent and utilities. The voucher is renewable and highly portable, meaning the tenant can move with it to another apartment and even to another city. Vouchers are issued by HUD at the federal level but administered through local housing authorities. HUD's Shelter Plus Care vouchers and Supportive Housing Program funds are renewable contracts, available to agencies by application and usually coordinated through the local HUD Continuum of Care application process. (See www.HUD.gov for more details.)

In Canada, the government anticipates that people who apply for welfare or disability are poor and will need additional income for housing. Thus, the government allocates a shelter allowance to recipients of welfare or disability to help them pay rent. People on disability receive a higher allowance than those on welfare. This allowance may afford a placement in a "social housing" unit or a unit at the low end of the open rental market. The Canadian Mental Health Commission's At Home project is currently studying various ways to provide and expand housing options for people who are homeless with co-occurring disorders. If a PHF client is eligible but does not currently receive a shelter allowance, the program can facilitate the application process for this benefit and the funds can be sent directly to the landlord.

In both the U.S. Section 8 program and Canada's shelter allowance programs, PHF housing staff and clinical staff must work proactively with clients and landlords to help them maintain the reporting requirements and renewals that may be part of the housing subsidy. Program staffers assist as much as possible to help reduce the burden on the landlord and to eliminate any lapses in reimbursement. This includes reminding clients of annual lease renewals, recertification appointments, and inspections.

Other excellent potential sources of rental income support are state, provincial, and city departments of mental health and social services, as well as health authorities and housing authorities. Again, when applying for any rental funding, it is important to ensure that such funds are renewable or in other ways considered permanent funding to meet the needs of this chronically homeless population.

When clients graduate from the PHF program and no longer need rent support, these funds can be applied to the next client who enters the program.

Funding PHF's Support and Clinical Services

Often, PHF support and clinical services are initially funded through grants and then moved into mainstream funding sources such as Medicaid in the United States or the Health Authority in Canada. The funding required for these services depends on the population to be served, the size of the PHF program, and the availability of other providers.

As discussed earlier, two types of service teams are commonly found in the PHF model: intensive case management (ICM) teams for clients with moderate disorders and assertive community treatment (ACT) teams for those with more severe disorders. If an ICM version of the program is implemented, it is highly recommended that funds also be obtained to hire a part-time psychiatrist to work with that team.

If an ACT team is used, funding should be sought for a part-time nurse practitioner or physician to provide primary health care. Whichever service team model is used, program staff should learn what additional services clients will need and should develop relationships with the providers of these services.

Important Budgetary Considerations

When implementing a PHF program, it is optimal to receive grants or contracts to fully fund the program during the first year. Even if the long-term goal is to transfer the program costs to an insurance payer like Medicaid or the National Health Plan, program planners must be careful to correctly project the program costs, the rate of client enrollment, and other aspects of program growth to accurately predict the level of funding needed for the all-important implementation year and for its subsequent ongoing operations.

There are usually more costs associated with operating a PHF program than can be anticipated. Many typical costs are listed in the sample budget for a PHF program's ACT team in a large U.S. city (see appendix D). For example, who will pay when clients are referred and have no money or benefits? Who will pay when clients have nothing to eat and no place to stay? Who will pay when housed clients lose keys or when their furniture breaks or their apartment needs to be exterminated for bed bugs? Who will pay for transportation when a client's relative dies and he or she wants to attend the funeral or when a client has a job interview and needs decent clothing? These are just a few reasons each PHF program requires a "client emergency fund."

The main point is to anticipate and obtain funding for what the program will actually cost. Judging by the thirty-plus studies on the cost savings of PHF programs (see appendix A), it is easy to make the case for adequate funding: the PHF program serves clients who would remain homeless and ill without it, costing the government many times more. PHF allows these same people to receive decent housing and excellent support services at a fraction of the price of high usage of public services.

Launching a PHF Program

When funding is secured, there are many tasks associated with starting a PHF program. *Remember that PHF programs have very brief start-up periods, on average about three months from the time funding is received, requiring knowledge and swift action on the part of program managers.*

Many internal program operations must be completed before a PHF program is implemented. Among them are these six:

1. **Job posting, interviewing, and hiring.** As emphasized in earlier chapters, the key to program success is hiring the right people. Hire for values; you can teach the skills. Hire people who are intelligent, warm, and compassionate, who understand and value social justice and harm reduction, and who embrace the PHF program philosophy. It is very useful if they are excellent clinicians who have worked with this population, especially in a "treatment first, then housing" model, so they understand why that approach fails the people whom PHF serves. If the long-term plan is to obtain a license and bill Medicaid, consider licensing and credentialing issues among potential staff. *Be sure to hire peer specialists for appropriate staff positions.*

2. **Accessible office space.** Rent enough space for the team—space enough for work stations and several offices, one large conference room for team meetings, an office for the team leader, and an office or offices for confidential interviews. Plan for a large welcoming reception area (with coffee and magazines) for clients to wait or meet and talk with each other. Use the conference room for client group meetings or for therapeutic, educational, or social purposes.

3. **Phone system and communication system.** PHF is field work, and every staff member needs a cell phone or wireless device, a computer, a Web-based clinical MIS system, and access to printers and other equipment.

4. **Vehicles.** Two, three, or more vehicles are needed, depending on the size of the team and availability of public transportation in the area in which the team is working. Another option is to include funding in the budget so staff can be reimbursed for using their own vehicles. Remember that 70 to 90 percent of a team's time is spent seeing clients in the field.

5. **Policy and procedure manuals.** Such PHF program manuals include guidance and information on everything from the referral process to intake to finding housing for clients and processes for moving clients into apartments.

6. **Training.** Start-up is an excellent opportunity to train staff on the PHF model, harm reduction, Motivational Interviewing, obtaining benefits for clients, safety in the field, and other topics.

Client Referrals

During the start-up phase of PHF program implementation, it is important to meet with people who will be potential sources for client referrals. These meetings should include a description of the PHF program and the clients the program seeks to serve. Agencies or programs that are potential referral sources include shelters, drop-in centers, hospital emergency rooms, police, detox centers, soup kitchens, and other community services.

Prospective program implementers should also meet with the agencies to which they will be referring or bringing clients. (It may be helpful to meet with the local staff of housing authorities and social welfare agencies, the bank employees who will handle client accounts, health clinic staff, and so on.)

Building a Network of Landlords

In earlier stages of program implementation, the program's housing specialist and team leader should develop relationships with community landlords. Learn which landlords in the community are currently renting units to other government programs that work with special populations such as older people, families, or people living with HIV.

Learn about community forums, landlord association or real estate-related meetings, community organization meetings, and other community events where one might meet prospective PHF landlords. Explain the PHF program, discuss the leasing arrangement, the rent payments, and so on, so that when the first client is enrolled, much of this preliminary work has already been completed.

Preferred Vendors

In the first year, many purchases are necessary: office furnishings and equipment as well as client household goods. A program that serves seventy-five clients will probably spend more than $100,000 on modest apartment furniture and appliances. This is a significant account, providing the PHF program considerable leverage in negotiating a very good deal for purchasing the furniture for its clients' apartments.

Once a vendor or vendors are selected, it is a good idea to create a catalog with a variety of furniture options, so clients can choose the furniture they want. This way, furniture can be ordered and delivered efficiently. Staff can also accompany clients to the local preselected vendors to purchase their housewares, sheets and towels, and other items.

The Important First Year—and Beyond

PHF program implementation and the first year of operation are by far the busiest times in a PHF program. *Everyone* is on a steep learning curve—staff, clients, landlords, and housing and governmental agencies. It is a year with multiple and endless tasks that require exceptional organizational skills. It is also one of the more emotional phases in the life of the program, because no one can anticipate anyone's behavior. There is no predicting which of the clients will succeed and which may lose their first apartment.

There are enormous ups and downs in PHF. Every day is different. A great deal of good is done, and good will abounds as client after client—homeless, exhausted, and in a mild state of disbelief—enters into a furnished apartment and sits down on his or her own bed for the first time in years!

Chapter 8 Summary

These are necessary elements for implementing a PHF program:

1. The leadership of the agency, the executive director, and the board of directors must support adopting the model.

2. The staff must see the PHF program as a solution for a group of clients who are currently not well served by existing services.

3. Leadership and staff must embrace the core idea of housing offered as a fundamental and unconditional right rather than a privilege that must be earned through demonstrating compliance with treatment or program rules.

4. Leadership and staff must learn and embrace a harm-reduction model in working with co-occurring disorders.

5. Ideally, new funding must be identified to implement the PHF program. A PHF program requires two sources of funding:

    a. Rental support to rent available apartments at fair market value

    b. Funds for the program's support and clinical services (either ACT or ICM, depending on the population to be served)

In the United States and Canada, the federal government is the largest source of rental funding. PHF support and clinical services are usually initially funded through grants and then moved into mainstream funding like Medicaid in the United States or the Health Authority in Canada. The funding required for PHF support and services depends on the population to be served, the size of the PHF program, and the availability of other providers.

Start-up program considerations: There are many internal program operations that must be completed before a PHF program is implemented, including hiring of staff, renting accessible office space, putting a phone and communication system in place, arranging for necessary vehicles, developing policy and procedure manuals, training staff, and building a network of landlords and preferred vendors.

Pathways Housing First Training Institute

As we mentioned in this manual's introduction—and as is no doubt even clearer to you now—the PHF program is a complex clinical and housing intervention that requires practice and supervision. This manual offers program fundamentals, but those who plan to introduce a PHF program into their own agency or community will require additional and more specific direction.

Specialized technical guidance on how to design, fund, start, operate, or evaluate a PHF program is available at the Pathways Housing First Training Institute, where Dr. Sam Tsemberis serves as the lead trainer and principal consultant. Other Institute faculty include Juliana Walker, director of training, and Christy Respress, director of programs, as well as experts in housing, clinical services, grant writing, research, and evaluation. The PHF Training Institute offers numerous courses on a range of topics, which are listed at the Pathways to Housing Web site at www .pathwaystohousing.org.

In addition, individual consultations are available at Pathways' offices or at your own site and typically take one or two days. The PHF Training Institute also offers the opportunity for ongoing consultation at regular intervals. The same individualized services can also be delivered via conference calls or video conferencing. To ensure the highest success rates for your program, the PHF Training Institute can provide a Housing First fidelity assessment and evaluation based on the PHF Fidelity Checklist. (See appendix C-5).

Prospective program implementers are also invited to visit Pathways in action at one of its sites in New York, Philadelphia, Washington DC, or Burlington, Vermont. This visit can be tailored to meet specific needs and allows visiting clinicians to join a morning meeting, visit several client apartments, view a client group, and meet with Dr. Tsemberis or senior staff for an individualized question-and-answer session. Contact the Pathways National Office at 212-289-0000, or e-mail us at info@pathwaystohousing.org to arrange a visit or to obtain more information.

Research and Evaluation

THIS APPENDIX REVIEWS SCIENTIFIC EVIDENCE about the quantity, quality, and cost-effectiveness of the Pathways Housing First (PHF) program in several cities. Some of the programs studied have used assertive community treatment (ACT) teams as the service modality; others have used intensive case management (ICM) teams. Most, however, used the model of independent scattered-site apartments with off-site support services. The results presented here provide uniform evidence that, when operated correctly, the PHF program helps end homelessness while supporting people with mental health and addiction problems.

Pathways Housing First as an Evidence-Based Practice

How does a particular practice or program achieve status as an "evidence-based practice"? It occurs when multiple empirically sound research studies—all of which are published in peer-reviewed journals—report that a practice or program has a consistently significant positive impact on a target population and that there are few or no negative effects.

In terms of Pathways Housing First, the research evidence includes a wide range of studies conducted by an array of investigators in various cities. PHF staff conducted some studies. In others, PHF staff collaborated with independent university researchers. In some cases, independent researchers, operating under contracts issued by government agencies or universities, conducted the studies.

After conducting a peer review of studies reporting on PHF's practices and impact, the U.S. Substance Abuse and Mental Health Services Administration (SAMHSA) listed Pathways Housing First as an evidence-based practice, or EBP. It is important to repeat that PHF also uses a number of other compatible EBPS developed by SAMHSA. These EBPS can be found on SAMHSA's Web site under Integrated Dual Disorders Treatment, Illness Management Recovery, and Supported Employment. (See www.nrepp.samhsa.gov/programfulldetails.asp?PROGRAM_ID=195.)

New York City's Pathways to Housing, Inc. has conducted ongoing program evaluations ever since it began serving clients, including several longitudinal multi-site comparison and cost studies. A bibliography of research evidence is available on the Pathways to Housing Web site. (See www.pathwaystohousing.org/Articles /Research.html.) The general findings are highlighted below:

- The vast majority of individuals served by PHF meet the definition of "chronically homeless" that is used by the U.S. Department of Housing and Urban Development. This definition applies to people who have been literally homeless (i.e., staying "on the streets" or in shelters) for a year or more or have been intermittently in and out of homelessness, shelters, hospitals, or jails for a year or more.

- PHF can successfully house nearly all persons with multiple diagnoses, including those that encompass mental health, addiction, and health issues.

- PHF often accepts people into the program who have been rejected by other residential or supportive housing providers.

- PHF can house people more quickly than other programs can because it does not require psychiatric treatment or sobriety as a precondition for housing.

- PHF clients relocate less often and have greater residential stability than people served by other residential providers.

- PHF has low attrition rates, meaning that clients retain their housing in the long run. Research shows that PHF maintains a success rate of

85 percent over a period of five years. Other models and providers show much greater attrition.

- PHF's comprehensive services cost less than other residential services or acute care services used by people who remain homeless.

- PHF's comprehensive program (which includes housing subsidies and services) costs less per day ($57) than a night at a shelter ($73). For those individuals not being served by any program, PHF's model is far less expensive. When homeless individuals find themselves in jail, the emergency room, or in a psychiatric hospital, costs run as high as $519 for an ER visit and $1,185 for a day in a hospital.

Pathways Housing First: Demonstrated Effectiveness

An ever-growing body of evidence shows the effectiveness of Pathways Housing First in ending homelessness. In particular, PHF helps promote housing stability, reduce service use, decrease costs, and improve quality of life.

Housing Retention and Stability

Studies show that PHF clients quickly achieve stable housing and retain that housing.

1. A randomized controlled trial of people who were literally homeless showed that after one year, clients in Pathways Housing First (the experimental group) spent 85 percent of their time stably housed. Clients in the services-as-usual group (the control group) spent less than 25 percent of their time stably housed (Tsemberis, Gulcur, and Nakae 2004).

    Furthermore, after two years, PHF clients still spent approximately 80 percent of their time stably housed, compared with only 30 percent for the control group (see figure 1).

    Housing First tenants also reduced the proportion of time they spent homeless from approximately 55 percent at baseline to 12 percent at one year and less than 5 percent after two years (see figure 2).

Figure 1.
Proportion of Time Spent in Stable Housing

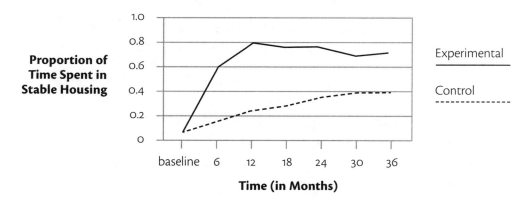

Reductions in homelessness were significantly slower and less dras-
tic for the control group, whose members were homeless approximately
50 percent of the time at baseline, 27 percent at one year, and 25 percent
after two years (Tsemberis, Gulcur, and Nakae 2004).

2. A randomized controlled trial of long-term shelter residents found
   that those assigned to Pathways Housing First obtained permanent, independent housing at higher rates than those assigned to a

Figure 2.
Proportion of Time Spent Homeless

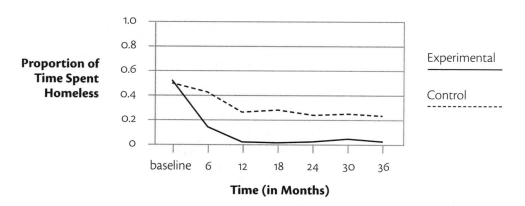

services-as-usual control group. Additionally, most clients housed by PHF agencies retained their housing over the course of four years. In fact, *78 percent of clients in the PHF program remained housed over that period* (Stefancic and Tsemberis 2007).

3. A randomized controlled trial in Chicago found that 60 percent of persons in a PHF program were stably housed at 18 months, compared with only 15 percent of persons assigned to usual care (Sadowski 2008; Bendixen 2008).

4. In a study using archival data, housing retention rates for Pathways Housing First tenants were compared to those of tenants in New York supportive housing programs that required treatment and sobriety as a precondition to housing. The study found that after five years, 88 percent of clients in the PHF program remained housed, compared to 47 percent of clients in the more traditional housing programs (Tsemberis and Eisenberg 2000).

5. A cross-site study of programs funded through the Collaborative Initiative to End Chronic Homeless demonstrated that high housing retention rates could be achieved across diverse contexts. At least *seven of the eleven programs funded used the Pathways' Housing First model and approximately 80 percent of clients were stably housed after one year* (Rosenheck et al. 2007).

6. A HUD cross-site study of three Pathways Housing First programs found that *84 percent of PHF clients were in permanent housing at baseline. That percentage remained unchanged one year later* (HUD 2007).

7. A single-site study in Philadelphia documented that *after approximately two years, 84 percent of clients in the PHF program were maintaining apartments in the community* (Dunbeck 2006).

8. A single-site study in Rhode Island documented that PHF clients had *a 78 percent housing retention rate over 18 months* (Hirsch and Glasser 2008).

Reductions in Service Use

Studies consistently demonstrate that Pathways Housing First is associated with a decline in emergency room visits, hospitalizations, incarcerations, and shelter stays. These findings strongly suggest that PHF is a lower-cost, more effective approach than traditional programs.

1. A randomized controlled trial in New York City found that people assigned to Pathways Housing First spent significantly less time in psychiatric hospitals compared to clients assigned to services-as-usual (Gulcur et al. 2003).

2. A randomized controlled trial in Chicago found that people in Pathways Housing First "used half as many nursing home days and were nearly two times less likely to be hospitalized or use emergency rooms" as compared to a usual care group over 18 months (Sadowski 2008; Bendixen 2008).

3. A pre-post study in Denver documented reductions in institutional acute care among homeless people after they enrolled in Pathways Housing First. The study found that PHF clients decreased their emergency room use by 73 percent, their inpatient stays by 66 percent, their detox use by 82 percent, and their incarceration rates by 76 percent (Perlman and Parvensky 2006).

4. A pre-post study in Rhode Island documented declines in hospital and jail stays, as well as declines in emergency room visits, after clients enrolled in Pathways Housing First. The study found that "In the year prior to entering supported housing, the formerly chronically homeless individuals spent a combined total of 534 nights in hospitals, [spent] 919 nights in jail, and had 177 emergency room visits. In contrast, the newly housed individuals had a combined total of only 149 nights in hospitals, 149 jail nights, and 75 emergency room visits in the first year of housing" (Hirsch and Glasser 2008).

5. A pre-post study in Seattle documented reductions in various services after clients enrolled in one of two Pathways Housing First

programs. When compared to data from the year before admission, PHF clients in one program decreased jail bookings by 52 percent and jail days by 45 percent. Additionally, admissions to a sobering center fell by 96 percent, EMS paramedic interventions fell by 20 percent, and visits to a medical center fell by 33 percent (HUD 2007).

Clients in the other PHF program reduced their medical respite days by 100 percent, their inpatient visits to a medical center by 83 percent, their emergency room visits by 74 percent, their jail days by 18 percent, and their admissions to a sobering center by 97 percent (Srebnik 2007).

6. A pre-post study of Pathways Housing First in Massachusetts demonstrated that in the year following enrollment in PHF, clients' inpatient hospitalizations fell by 77 percent and emergency room visits declined by 83 percent (Meschede 2004).

In-house data collection in Calgary indicated that there were significant reductions across the board for supportive community services. The highlights include these figures:

- 75 percent reduction in psychiatric hospitalizations

- 65 percent reduction in police contacts

- 80 percent reduction in ambulance transports

- 56 percent reduction in the number of days clients spent in Remand (In the United Kingdom and in Canada, a "remand center" is a place of detention where accused people awaiting criminal trial are detained.)

Decreased Costs

Studies consistently show that Pathways Housing First is associated with decreased costs.

1. In New York City, a randomized controlled trial of people deemed literally homeless showed that, from baseline to two-year follow-up, *clients in Pathways Housing First accrued significantly lower supportive housing and services costs than clients in services-as-usual* (Gulcur et al. 2003).

2. A pre-post study in Denver estimated that enrollment in Pathways Housing First was associated with a net cost savings of $4,745 per person per year (Perlman and Parvensky 2006).

3. A pre-post study in Rhode Island estimated that enrollment in Pathways Housing First was associated with a net cost savings of $8,839 per person per year (Hirsch and Glasser 2008).

4. A pre-post study in Seattle estimated that two Pathways Housing First programs were associated with an aggregate reduction in cost of services of $3.2 million (HUD 2007; Srebnik 2007).

5. A randomized controlled trial in Chicago concluded that *"health care savings far exceed the costs of the Housing [First] intervention"* (National AIDS Housing Coalition 2008).

Improvements in Quality of Life and Other Outcomes

Studies consistently find that Pathways Housing First is associated with greater client choice, greater satisfaction, improved quality of life, and improvements in other clinical and personal domains.

1. A randomized controlled trial found that *clients assigned to Pathways Housing First reported higher ratings of perceived choice compared to those in services-as-usual* (Greenwood et al. 2005). Although program assignment did not have a direct effect on psychiatric symptoms, perceived choice led to a decrease in psychiatric symptoms. This relationship was partially mediated by mastery (the perception of personal control).

2. A qualitative study found that PHF *clients living in their own apartments reported experiencing conditions that foster a sense of control, allow for the enactment of daily routines, impart a sense of privacy,*

and provide a foundation from which clients can engage in identity construction—all of which are conditions indicative of a stable home (Padgett 2007).

3. A Rhode Island study found that in the year before moving into an apartment, 93 percent of potential clients reported that they were "very dissatisfied" with their housing situation. This number immediately changed when they became clients. *By the time of their first program interviews, 78 percent reported that they were "very satisfied."*

   Also, while homeless, nearly half of all potential clients rated their health as "poor" or "very poor." Two-thirds of potential clients said that physical or mental health disabilities had limited their ability to interact with those they felt close to. However, once enrolled in the program, *nearly half of all clients rated their health as "good" or "very good," and only one-third felt that their disabilities now limited their social interactions* (Hirsch and Glasser 2008).

4. A Pathways Housing First program in Massachusetts found that *"overall quality of life improved dramatically for all PHF residents after leaving the shelter, including increased sense of independence, control of their lives, and satisfaction with their housing"* (Meschede 2004).

5. Compared to clients in community residences over an eighteen-month period, *those in supported housing (Housing First and another supported housing program) reported greater satisfaction in terms of autonomy and economic viability* (Siegel et al. 2006).

6. A qualitative study of clients in a randomized controlled trial found that for most Pathways Housing First clients, *entering housing after a long period of homelessness was associated with improvements in several psychological aspects of integration (e.g., a sense of fitting in and belonging) as well as feelings of being "normal"* or part of the mainstream human experience (Yanos et al. 2004).

7. An evaluation in Philadelphia compared clients in Pathways Housing First to a group of people receiving services but no housing. *Of the clients in PHF, 79 percent showed improvement in mental health (the comparison group was 20 percent), 57 percent showed improvement on substance use (the comparison group was 15 percent), and 84 percent showed improvement in overall life status (the comparison group was 50 percent)* (Dunbeck 2006).

Some Administrative Considerations

CREATING YOUR **POLICIES AND PROCEDURES MANUAL** prior to starting a PHF program is extremely important. It is equally important to conduct regular reviews and be willing to make changes and add to staff as needed. From the inception of a PHF program, consider establishing procedures for these areas:

- intake

- time frames for completing standard documents, such as goal plans and assessments

- discharges

- petty cash

- purchasing items for clients

- handling clients' funds

- reimbursement for travel

- critical incident management

- scheduling staff time off

- supervision expectations and housing-related items, such as who maintains copies of clients' keys and ensures they are handled appropriately

- move-in and move-out day

Depending on what your agency already has in place, many of these procedures can be adapted for new programs.

Keep in mind these basics when starting up a PHF team:

Hiring: The team, *not* Human Resources, needs to have the final say when hiring team members. Each candidate should be interviewed by the team leader and the team. He or she should spend some time doing home visits with the team so that he or she understands the nature of the work. The person should be able to demonstrate a commitment to recovery and Pathways Housing First ideals.

Transportation: There needs to be a plan for transporting team members to see the clients, especially after they are housed. Transportation needs to be easily accessible and not a barrier to providing services. One option is to provide a number of vehicles for team members. In this case, someone needs to be assigned as a point person to make sure the keys are being logged in and out, mileage is recorded, routine maintenance is handled, and all insurance and administrative functions occur regularly.

Petty cash: There is always a need to have a small amount of cash on hand. You may need to take a client out to lunch, put him or her in a hotel for a night, or provide a clean pair of socks and underwear. When working with 60 to 100 individuals living in their own apartments across the city or town, something is bound to come up that requires having some spare money on hand.

Client emergency funds: Establish a client emergency fund for the team (estimate the total at approximately $300 per client—but this will vary by client). This is simply a pool of money renewed annually so the team can efficiently address client-related emergencies, ranging from buying clothing and food for the new applicant coming in from the street to buying a bus ticket for an emergency trip to visit a family member.

Furniture and apartment repairs fund: This fund is to replace furniture and pay for the cost of making repairs to apartments when it is best not to let the landlord make them.

Establishing relationships with local vendors: It can be very helpful to build relationships with the local furniture company, grocery store, food bank, department store, and so on. It is especially helpful to establish accounts at these stores and have them bill the program on a monthly basis, saving time and letting the team run more efficiently.

Building community partnerships: To identify and effectively serve PHF clients, the program builds working alliances with local providers. To help identify clients ideally suited for this intervention, establish referral procedures with the following:

- drop-in centers

- shelters

- emergency rooms

- the police

- detox centers

- soup kitchens

- other street-level services for people who are homeless

Once a client is housed, the program needs to work with an array of agencies that provide services in the client's community, including medical, dental, and eye care clinics, libraries, places of worship, and potential employers.

Appendix C

Sample Forms

Appendix C-1: The ACT Team Morning Meeting Description and Checklist

Appendix C-2: Furniture List and Client Shopping List

Appendix C-3: Pre-Move-In Apartment Readiness Checklist

Appendix C-4: Use and Occupancy Agreement

Appendix C-5: Pathways Housing First Program Fidelity:
The Essential Ingredients Checklist

The ACT Team Morning Meeting Description and Checklist

See chapter 5 for more information and sample forms used by ACT teams in a Pathways to Housing context.

ACT Team Morning Meeting Description

Purpose

The ACT team's morning meeting is designed for efficiency. The goal is to share the most recent clinical information and plan the work for the day. This is not the time to have a case conference.

Crucial Points of the Morning Meeting

The morning meeting is often the only time when all staff members are together. It is critical at each meeting to read each client's name and the date of the team's last contact with the person. Reading each name ensures that no one is missed.

The meeting should last no more than 45 to 60 minutes. The idea is to be efficient and accurate in the communication that will allow the team to start their work in the field with the clients as soon as possible. Everyone on the team has a unique and important perspective to offer. Everyone's input is valued; no one person should dominate the meeting. The driving force of communication should be the progress note that is being read.

The meeting is structured around several duties that are shared by team members.

1. **Contact log:** The person reading this log is keeping the pace of the meeting (this duty rotates daily). The person reads aloud each client name and date of last contact—and, if the last contact was the day before, the progress note log must be read aloud.

2. **Progress note log:** The person managing this log reads aloud all notes that were generated from the team activities the day before. (This is why that the progress note documentation must be completed before the morning meeting.) This duty also rotates daily.

3. **The boards:** One person is standing at the dry-erase boards—the weekly and monthly schedules—filling in any appointments that were not placed on the board before the meeting, and reminding the team of the existing appointments for that day. (This duty also rotates daily.)

4. **The daily schedule:** The program assistant is compiling the daily schedule from the items shown on the weekly schedule, plus any other visits or activities that are decided during morning meeting. At the end of the meeting, the program assistant copies the daily schedule and ensures that everyone has a copy of the entire schedule. This allows for transparency and for people to know where to reach other team members for assistance if needed. Everyone should be able to perform this function in case the program assistant is not available.

5. **On-call log:** The person on call also reports any activity from the on-call log that they are maintaining while they are on call.

ACT Morning Meeting Checklist

		Yes	No
1.	The daily meeting begins on time.		
2.	All staff are on time (no one has to be asked to join the meeting).		
3.	No other work is being done during the meeting.		
4.	Meeting begins with a pleasant introduction.		
5.	Everyone is actively listening.		
6.	Staff body language is positive/attentive and there are no displays of sarcasm.		
7.	Respectful, "person-first" language is used when referring to the service recipients.		
8.	Log entries are complete prior to the meeting.		
9.	Person reading the contact log is keeping the meeting focused (duty rotated daily).		
10.	Progress notes are read by one staff person (duty rotated daily).		
11.	Progress notes are speaking for staff.		
12.	There are no sidebar conversations during the meeting.		
13.	Topics requiring clinical discussion are tabled until the end of the meeting or the next clinical meeting.		
14.	One staff person is assigned to make entries on the dry-erase boards (duty rotated daily).		
15.	Notes indicate the goal that was the driving force for the outreach or visit.		
16.	Notes indicate what clinical interventions the staff used during the visit.		
17.	Notes indicate that shared decision making is evident.		
18.	Notes indicate the person's response to the staff's intervention(s).		
19.	Notes indicate the plan of when to see the person next and for what specific reason.		
20.	The meeting observer can clearly see that goals are being worked on, such as vocational, independence, school, social, housing, and so on.		

(continued)

ACT Morning Meeting Checklist (continued)

		Yes	No
21.	A comprehensive schedule for all staff is generated and distributed at the close of the meeting.		
22.	The meeting observer can clearly see that Motivational Interviewing/ cognitive behavioral therapy and Stages of Change techniques are being used and documented.		
23.	Everyone agrees to assignments/visits by the end of the meeting. (Some teams assign visits after each person is discussed; some teams make all assignments at the close of the meeting.)		
24.	The meeting observer can clearly see that communications with other service providers are collaborative, helping to enhance the relationship with the team.		
25.	Decisions are made by the team and not by a select few.		
26.	The Director provides system-wide information, actively encourages innovation/creativity, and provides assistance when systems break down.		
27.	Visits are not made just to deliver medication; additional goals and interventions are also addressed.		
28.	The meeting has a clear end point: no staff person leaves until all decisions are made.		

Supports

		Yes	No
1.	Team has all staff present for the meeting (all positions).		
2.	Team is empowered to make clinical decisions necessary to complete work.		
3.	Team has cars or other transport sufficient to conduct the work.		
4.	All cell phones are in good working order.		
5.	Documentation is filed and maintained so as to have ready access.		
6.	Assistance funds are readily available.		
7.	Other technology is in place and in good working order, e.g., laptops, computers, phones, and so on.		

Furniture List and Client Shopping List

Move-in Furniture Packages for One-Bedroom and Studio Apartments

One-bedroom apartment:

Full-size bed
Dresser
Couch or love seat and chair
Three-piece coffee table and end table set
Dinette set with four chairs
Television with stand
Telephone
Lamps

Studio apartment:

Single bed or sofa bed
Dresser
Love seat
Three-piece coffee table and end table set
Dinette set with two chairs

Television with stand
Telephone
Lamps

Client Shopping List

Bathroom

Shower curtain
Shower liner
Shower curtain rings
Bathroom rug set
Towels
Wash cloths
Garbage can set
Bathmat
Toilet paper
Toothbrush
Toothpaste

Bedroom

Full-size sheets
Blanket
Pillows
Hangers

Kitchen

Pots and pans
Silverware
Silverware drawer organizer
Dishes
Garbage can
Dish drainer/rack

Can opener
Cooking utensils
Knives
Dishwashing liquid
Dish towel
Dish cloths
Pot holders

Cleaning

Sponges
Scouring cleanser/Disinfecting spray
Broom
Dust pan
Mop
Bucket
Garbage bags

Extras (can be purchased if client has food stamps)

Paper towels
Antenna
Iron
Ironing board
Toaster
Shopping/push cart

Pre-Move-In Apartment Readiness Checklist

	Yes	No	Notes
Address:			
Name of tenant:			
Furniture			
Bed			
Dresser			
Sofa			
Coffee table and two end tables			
TV			
TV stand			
Dinette table			
2 or 4 dinette chairs			
Lamps			

(continued)

	Yes	No	Notes
Is there electricity in the apartment?			
Do the lights work in the...			
Entryway?			
Bathroom?			
Kitchen?			
Bedroom?			
Is there a stove?			
Does it work?			
Is there a refrigerator?			
Does it work?			
Are there gates in the apartment? *(Gates should be on all first-floor windows and on windows at fire escape.)*			
Are there shades on all windows?			
Is there a...			
Front door key?			
Mailbox key?			
Top lock key?			
Bottom lock key?			
Phone jack?			
Top lock?			
Bottom lock?			

Name of person reviewing form:

Date:

Use and Occupancy Agreement

Agreement made on, by, and between Action Realty/Pathways To Housing, Inc, having a principal office at 186 East 123rd Street, New York, New York 10035 and _____ [client's name].

- Pathways is the Tenant in and under certain Lease dated _____ [date of lease] for the apartment number _____ located in a building having an address of _____[building address].

- The landlord in and under the Lease is _____ [landlord's name].

- The term of the Lease begins on _____ [date] and ends on _____ [date].

- It is the intention of the parties hereto to provide stable, permanent housing for the Client as part of a specially funded program (The Pathways program). Consequently, if the Lease can be renewed, Pathways intends to so renew the Lease and the Term will end at the expiration of any and all such renewal terms (the "Expiration Date").

- It is the intention of the parties hereto that the Apartment be used and occupied by the Client, under the terms and conditions set forth herein.

1. Subject to Lease

The Client represents that he or she has read the Lease, a copy of which has been and is available in Action Realty's office. All of the terms, covenants, and provisions of the Lease are hereby incorporated into this Agreement by reference. The Client acknowledges and agrees to be bound by all such terms, covenants, and provisions and agrees not to violate any of the terms of the Lease in any way. This Agreement is subject to the Lease; if for any reason whatsoever the Lease shall expire, terminate, otherwise come to an end, or shall not be renewed, this Agreement shall simultaneously expire, terminate, and come to an end.

2. The Term

    a. Provided the Client complies with the terms, covenants, and provisions of the Lease and this Agreement, Pathways and the Client agree that the Client shall be entitled to use and occupy the Apartment during the term.

    b. Pathways expects that the Lease will be continuously renewed. For so long as the Lease remains in effect, this Agreement shall be automatically renewed, provided the Client abides by the terms and conditions of this Agreement.

    c. If the Lease shall not be renewed, the Client must vacate the Apartment on or prior to the Expiration Date.

    d. If the Client is discharged from the Pathways program for cause, this Agreement shall terminate and the Client must vacate the Apartment on the date of discharge.

    e. If the Client graduates from the Pathways program, this Agreement shall terminate on the date of graduation, and the Client's continued occupancy of the Apartment, if so desired, is at the absolute discretion of Pathways and the Landlord.

    f. If Pathways deems it necessary for its mission and to carry out its charitable purposes, upon not less than 60 days notice, Pathways may require the Client to vacate the Apartment, but in such event Pathways shall provide alternate housing to the Client.

3. Use

The Client shall use the Apartment solely as a private residential dwelling as his/her primary residence. The Apartment may be used and occupied solely by the Client. The Apartment may not be used as a primary residence by any other individuals, except with the expressed approval of Pathways.

4. Rules and Regulations

As part of the Pathways program, Pathways is permitting the Client to use and occupy the Apartment, and the Client agrees to be bound by the following Rules and Regulations:

a. The Client allows a Pathways Service Coordinator access to the Apartment every two weeks.

b. The Client meets with the Service Coordinator or team member once a week.

c. The Client may not sell any furniture that is provided by Pathways program.

d. The Client's failure to abide by the Rules and Regulations implemented by either Pathways or the Landlord may be grounds for immediate termination of this Agreement and eviction from the Apartment.

5. Objectionable Conduct

a. The Client shall not engage in any objectionable conduct whatsoever. "Objectionable conduct" means behavior by the Client or any guests of the Client, that makes, or will make, the Apartment or the Building dangerous, hazardous, unsanitary, and/or detrimental to other tenants or occupants of the Building. It also means any conduct by the Client or by any guests of the Client that interferes with the right of the other tenants or occupants of the Building to quiet enjoyment of their apartments. Any violation of this paragraph shall constitute a substantial breach of this Agreement and will be grounds for immediate termination of this Agreement and eviction from the Apartment.

b. The following behaviors by the Client and any guests of the Client in, at, or on the Apartment or the Building are strictly prohibited and will be grounds for immediate termination of this Agreement and eviction from the Apartment:

1. The possession or use of any illegal weapon.

2. The creation of severe disturbances, or behavioral problems that interfere with the orderly operation of the Pathways program or interfere with the quiet enjoyment of any other tenant or occupant of the Building.

3. Any behavior that poses imminent risk of death or physical harm to any other tenant or occupant of the Building or any other person.

4. Any behavior that causes damage to the property of Pathways or that of the Landlord or any other tenant or occupant of the Building.

6. Rent; Utilities

a. Where Pathways is the representative-payee of the Client, Pathways shall deduct (as the Client's contribution toward rent and housing support services) thirty percent (30%) of his/her gross monthly income. Where the Client is their own payee, the Client shall pay to Pathways (as the Client's contribution toward rent and housing support services) thirty percent (30%) of his/her net (after tax) monthly income.

b. The Client agrees to pay directly to the utility provider, or authorizes Pathways to pay on his/her behalf, all utility bills, including without limitation, electricity, telephone, gas , water, cable, and any other utilities used in the Apartment.

7. Expiration of Term; Renewal

a. It is expressly understood and agreed that the Client's use and occupancy of the Apartment pursuant to this Agreement is for a term that is the shorter of one (1) year, or the time left on the term of the Lease. It is Pathways intention, however to provide stable, permanent housing for the Client. Consequently, provided (i) Pathways is entitled to and does renew the Lease, and (ii) the Client is in compliance with the provisions of this Agreement and with the Pathways program, then this Agreement shall be automatically renewed through the Expiration Date of each such renewal term of the Lease.

b. At the expiration of the term of this Agreement, including any renewal terms, the Client shall deliver the Apartment broom-clean and in good order and condition, except for reasonable wear and tear, and shall remove all of his/her personal property from the Apartment. Any of the Client's personal property that is left in the Apartment at the end of the term of this Agreement shall be deemed abandoned and Pathways shall have no responsibility for it.

c. If the Client is required to vacate the Apartment upon the Expiration Date of the Lease, and the last day of the Lease Term is a Saturday, Sunday, or State or Federal holiday, the term of this Agreement shall end on the prior business day.

d. It is agreed that Pathways, by entering into this Agreement, is not deprived of any legal or equitable remedy for obtaining possession of the Apartment in the event of the Client's failure to vacate the Apartment.

8. Assignment

This Agreement may not be assigned by the Client. The Client's failure to abide by the terms of this provision shall be grounds for immediate termination of this Agreement and eviction from the Apartment.

9. Fires and Casualty

The Client shall give Pathways prompt notice of fire, accident, damage, or any dangerous conditions in or about the Apartment and /or in or about the Building.

10. Repairs

a. The Client has inspected the Apartment and agrees to take the same in the present "as is" condition. In the event that any part of the Apartment shall fall into disrepair due to no fault of the Client, the Client shall promptly notify Pathways. Pathways shall take the appropriate measures to address the Client's repair concerns.

b. Wherever the need for repair results from his/her negligence or his/her guests' negligence, or intentional misconduct, normal wear and tear excepted, then the Client shall at his/her cost, make such repairs and replacements. If the Client fails to make a needed repair or replacement, Pathways may do so and shall thereafter make a payment arrangement with the Client for reimbursement. The Client shall be required to reimburse Pathways for its expenses.

11. Access

The Client shall permit the Landlord and its agents access into the Apartment in accordance with the Lease. Failure to permit such access and entry shall be deemed a material breach of this Agreement upon reasonable notice and at reasonable times. Both the Landlord and Pathways and their agents shall have immediate access into the Apartment in the event of emergency. The Client shall leave a duplicate key to the Apartment (and all entry doors to the Building) with his or her Pathways Service Coordinator.

12. Services

    a. In the event heat, hot and cold water, gas and electric service are not being supplied to the Apartment as required by the Lease, the Client shall promptly notify Pathways. Pathways is not responsible for any defect in such services.

    b. Pathways' intent is to supply basic household furnishing to meet client needs. Unless otherwise agreed to, such furniture and equipment is and remains the property of Pathways. The Client shall deliver same in good order and condition except for wear and tear, at the expiration of this Agreement.

Pets

If the Client would like to keep a pet in the Apartment, the Client must notify Pathways. Pathways will request permission from the Landlord or assist the client in requesting permission from the Landlord. Unless the Landlord gives such permission, pets are not allowed in the Apartment.

13. Indemnity

The Client acknowledges that Pathways is not and shall not be responsible to the Client for the any injury to the Client or damage occurring as a result of the Client's occupancy of the Apartment. The Client is responsible for any damage to the Apartment and any claims arising in connection with the Client's occupancy of the Apartment (including, without limitation, attorney's fees and disbursements). If Pathways incurs damages due to a claim of any nature whatsoever arising out of or in connection with the Client's occupancy of the Apartment under this Agreement, the Client will indemnify Pathways.

14. Notices

The Client agrees to promptly forward to Action Realty any notices, letters, or correspondence ("NOTICE") that he/she receives at the Apartment or otherwise from the Landlord.

15. Pathways Contact

Until further written notice, the Client's designated contact at Pathways shall be his/her Service Coordinator; any discussion about this Agreement shall be with the Service Coordinator; all Notices received by the Client shall be forwarded to the Service Coordinator; and any inquiries, questions, or problems associated with this Agreement shall be made, given, or directed to such Service Coordinator.

16. Full Agreement

The Client acknowledges that he/she has read this Agreement and understands its terms and conditions. There are no other agreements by or between the Client and Action Realty/Pathways regarding the Apartment. This Agreement may only be changed in writing, signed by both the Client and Action Realty/Pathways.

IN WITNESS WHEREOF, the parties hereto have executed this Agreement as of the date first above written.

ACTION REALTY/PATHWAYS TO HOUSING

By:
Title: ADMINISTRATIVE ASSISTANT
     ACTION REALTY/PATHWAYS TO HOUSING, INC.

CLIENT:
SIGNATURE:

Pathways Housing First Program Fidelity: The Essential Ingredients Checklist

THIS CHECKLIST IS COMPRISED OF ITEMS that most experts consider essential ingredients of the PHF program. These features are listed here as numbered items under five main headings: housing choice and structure, separation of housing and services, service philosophy, service array, and program structure. The checklist can be used to ensure that all of the important areas of the program are implemented and operational. (This checklist is not a fidelity measure; a fidelity assessment is conducted by outside experts who observe the team's work and conduct interviews with team members and consumers.) *Note:* This list applies to PHF programs using ACT teams (assertive community treatment). For programs using ICM teams (intensive case management), see the modifications listed below the table.

I. Housing Choice and Structure

1. Program participants have much choice in the location and other features of their housing.
2. Program helps participants move quickly into units of their choosing (under 6 weeks upon securing a housing subsidy).
3. Housing tenure is assumed to be permanent, with no actual or expected time limits other than those defined under a standard lease or occupancy agreement.
4. Program participants pay a reasonable amount of their income (less than 30 percent) for housing costs.

5. Program participants live in scattered-site private market housing which is otherwise available to people without psychiatric or other disabilities.

6. Program participants are not expected to share any living areas with other tenants.

II. Separation of Housing and Services

7. Program participants are not required to demonstrate housing readiness to gain access to housing units.

8. Continued tenancy is not linked in any way with adherence to clinical, treatment, or service provisions.

9. Program participants have legal rights to the unit, with no special provisions added to the lease or occupancy agreement.

10. Program offers participants who have lost their housing access to a new housing unit with no standardized limits on the number of relocations.

11. Program participants continue receiving program services even if they lose housing.

12. Program staff are not located at participants' residences and are mobile, with the ability to deliver services in locations of participants' choosing.

III. Service Philosophy

13. Program participants choose the type, sequence, and intensity of services on an ongoing basis.

14. Program participants with psychiatric disabilities are not required to take medication or participate in formal treatment activities.

15. Program participants with substance use disorders are not required to participate in formal treatment activities.

16. Program utilizes a harm-reduction approach to substance use (it does not require abstinence and works to reduce the negative consequences of use).

17. Staff consistently utilize principles of motivational interviewing in daily practice.

18. Program uses an array of techniques to engage participants who are difficult to engage.

19. Program does not engage in coercive activities to promote engagement or treatment adherence among participants.

20. Program conducts person-centered treatment planning.

21. Program systematically delivers specific interventions to address a broad range of life areas.

22. Program increases, and is a strong advocate for, participants' self-determination and independence in day-to-day activities.

IV. Service Array

23. Program offers services to help participants maintain housing, including assistance with subsidies, utility setup, neighborhood orientation, landlord relations, property management, budgeting, and shopping.

24. Psychiatric services are provided directly by the program.

25. Integrated, stage-wise substance use treatment is provided directly by the program.

26. Supported Employment services are provided directly by the program.

27. Nursing services are provided directly by the program.

28. Services supporting social integration are provided directly by the program.

29. Program responds to psychiatric or other crises twenty-four hours a day by phone and links participants to emergency services as necessary.

30. Program is involved in inpatient treatment admissions and works with inpatient staff to ensure proper discharge.

V. Program Structure

31. Program gives priority enrollment to individuals with multiple obstacles to housing stability.

32. Program consistently maintains a low participant/staff ratio (10:1), excluding the psychiatrist and administrative support.

33. Program has a minimum threshold of contact with participants to ensure safety and well-being.

34. Program staff function as a multidisciplinary team; clinicians know and work with all program participants.

35. Program staff meet frequently to plan and review services for each program participant.

36. Program uses a daily organizational meeting to conduct a brief, clinically relevant review of all participants and contacts in past twenty-four hours, and to develop a daily staff schedule.

37. Program has a staff member with professional status on team who meets local standards for certification as a peer specialist or meets specified qualifications.

38. Program offers participants opportunities for representation and input in program operations and policies.

Checklist Modifications for Programs Using ICM Teams

As noted above, these features apply directly to PHF programs operating ACT teams. For programs that use an ICM approach to services, modify the list this way:

- Items 24–28: Services specified here are not expected to be provided directly by the program; the program is evaluated on its ability to successfully broker the specified services.

- Item 32: Caseload ratios are increased to 15:1 or 20:1, depending on population served.

- Item 34: "Team approach" does not apply.

- Item 36: This item evaluates programs' weekly case review sessions.

Sources

Several items were taken directly or modified from other sources:

Items 4, 5, 7–9, 12, and 31: Permanent Supportive Housing KIT, fidelity scale. Source: Substance Abuse and Mental Health Services Administration (SAMHSA, 2010). *Permanent Supportive Housing: Evaluating Your Program.* DHHS Pub. No. SMA-10-4509, Rockville, MD: Center for Mental Health Services, SAMHSA, U.S. Department of Health and Human Services.

Items 29, 30, 32, 34, and 35: Assertive Community Treatment Fidelity Scale. Source: Substance Abuse and Mental Health Services Administration (SAMHSA, 2008). *Permanent Supportive Housing: Evaluating Your Program.* DHHS Pub. No. SMA-08-4344, Rockville, MD: Center for Mental Health Services, SAMHSA, U.S. Department of Health and Human Services.

Items 18, 20–22, 24–27, 36, and 37: Tool for Measurement of Assertive Community Treatment (TMACT). Source: Monroe-DeVita, M., Moser, L.L., and Teague, G.B. (2010). *The Tool for Measurement of Assertive Community Treatment (TMACT).* Unpublished measure.

Items 3, 13–15, and 23: Program Characteristics Measure. Source: Williams, V. F., Banks, S. M., Robbins, P. C., Oakley, D., and Dean, J. (2001). *Final Report on the Cross-Site Evaluation of the Collaborative Program to Prevent Homelessness.* Delmar, NY: Policy Research Associates.

Sample Budget

THIS SAMPLE BUDGET SHOWS THE APPROXIMATE ANNUAL COSTS of operating a Pathways Housing First program. It is offered as an illustration, not an actual budget; it lists the program costs that, in an ideal scenario, would all be funded. This budget shows the cost for an assertive community treatment (ACT) team serving 80 clients in their own furnished apartments in a large U.S. city, with salaries and rents estimated accordingly. Actual costs vary with location, program size, and service team (ICM teams have lower staffing costs, but housing and most other operation costs remain the same). As noted earlier, PFH programs are highly cost-effective when compared to other residential models, or to the costs of acute care services needed by clients who remain homeless.

The "PHF with Enhanced ACT Team" annual budget includes both clinical and housing staff (with additional funds to provide primary care through a full-time nurse practitioner and housing services through a housing specialist). Other support staff costs such as IT, HR, and accounting are also included. Other annual expenses are listed in the sections below. If you are launching a new program, see the "New PHF Program Start-up Costs" section as well. *Please note: These figures are approximate, based on 2010 market conditions. You would need to adjust costs to your locality and program size and type. These expenses are offered as a guide for anticipating the many small additional costs of running a PHF program.*

PHF with Enhanced ACT Team Clinical Services

*Asterisked staff roles would be included in an ideal, "enhanced" PHF ACT team.

ACT Team Member	Annual Salary (if full-time)	Staff FTEs (full-time equivalents)	Actual Salary Expense	
Team Leader	$65,000	1	$65,000	
Asst. Team Leader	45,000	1	45,000	
Nurse Practitioner*	85,000	1	85,000	
Psychiatrist	150,000	0.5	75,000	
R.N. Service Coordinator	70,000	1	70,000	
Service Coordinator	41,000	2	82,000	
Peer Specialists	35,000	2	70,000	
Housing Specialist*	45,000	1	45,000	
Program Admin. Asst.	35,000	1	35,000	
Bookkeeper/Jr. Accountant*	50,000	0.5	25,000	
HR Specialist*	50,000	0.1	5,000	
IT Specialist*	50,000	0.1	5,000	
Total Salaries		(Total FTEs: 11.2)	607,000	
Fringe Benefits			169,960	
Total Salaries and Fringe Benefits			$776,960	**$776,960**

Other Operating Expenses

Office rent	$54,500	
Communications expenses	12,000	
Insurance	20,000	
Vehicle leases	23,400	

Vehicle operating costs	22,500	
Service dollar expenses (client expenses)	20,000	
Client transportation	15,000	
Medication and pharmacological supplies	15,000	
Program activities	10,000	
Client living expenses	5,000	
Apartment maintenance, supplies, and outside contracts	50,000	
Furniture—replacement and turnover	10,000	
Replacement broker fees and security	10,000	
Moving expenses—relocations and turnover	5,000	
Billing software	25,000	
Office supplies	15,000	
Staff travel	7,000	
Conferences and meetings	6,000	
Office equipment rental: copiers	7,500	
Printing and postage	3,000	
Medical supplies	2,000	
Food	1,000	
Miscellaneous expenses	15,000	
Total Other Operating Expenses *(excluding administrative and supervisory)*	$353,900	**$353,900**
Administrative and Supervisory Expenses		
Administrative and Supervisory *(other staff and overhead expenses not itemized here)*	$75,000	**$75,000**
TOTAL ANNUAL BUDGET FOR EXISTING PHF PROGRAM: *(excluding new program start-up costs)*		**$1,205,860**

New PHF Program Start-up Costs *(for programs using tenant-based Section 8 vouchers)*		
Computers, servers, phone system	$25,400	
Office furniture	20,000	
Office equipment	5,000	
Initial client furniture purchases (80 apartments)	112,500	
Initial client move-in expenses (moving/supplies)	45,000	
Initial broker fees, year one only	75,000	
Initial client one-month security deposits	75,000	
Total New Program Start-Up Costs	**$357,900**	**$357,900**
TOTAL BUDGET for PHF Program Start-Up and First Year		**$1,563,760**

Awards Received by Pathways Housing First and Dr. Sam Tsemberis

Pathways to Housing, Inc. Featured Awards

In 2008, the Catalogue for Philanthropy featured Pathways DC as one of the best nonprofit programs in the greater metropolitan DC region.

In 2007, Pathways to Housing, Inc. was awarded the Excellence in Innovation Award from the National Council for Community Behavioral Healthcare, which represents 1,300 organizations providing treatment and rehabilitation to help people recover from mental illnesses and addiction disorders nationwide.

In 2006, Dr. Sam Tsemberis won the National Alliance to End Homelessness John E. Macy Award for Individual Achievement. As founder and executive director of Pathways to Housing, Inc., Dr. Tsemberis received this distinguished award for outstanding success with the Housing First model in New York City and the District of Columbia.

In 2005, the American Psychiatric Association presented Pathways to Housing, Inc. with its Gold Award (first place) for Community Mental Health Program for the "exemplary success of [its] Housing First program in the provision of permanent housing and treatment services for adults with severe mental illness and co-occurring substance use disorders."

Pathways New York Featured Awards

2002 **New York University, Division of Nursing:** Special Recognition Award

2002 **New York Association for Psychiatric Rehabilitation:** Marty Smith Memorial Award, for Outstanding Contribution to the Advancement of Services for People with Psychiatric Disabilities

2001 **National Alliance for the Mentally Ill NYC:** Special Achievement in Housing Award

Pathways DC Featured Awards

2009 **AmeriCorps:** Program Support and Leadership Award

2008 **Chronicle for Philanthropy:** Best small philanthropy in the Washington area

2007 **Consumer Leadership Forum:** for providing good consumer services

Awards Presented to Dr. Sam Tsemberis

2008 **Behavioral Healthcare:** Behavioral Healthcare Champion

2006 **National Alliance to End Homelessness:** Macy Award for Individual Achievement, Kennedy Center, Washington, DC

2005 **American Association of Psychiatric Administrators, New York:** Distinguished Psychiatric Administrator Award

2004 **Public Health Association of New York:** for Leadership and Advocacy that promotes public health

Two Testimonials

MY EARLIEST RECOLLECTIONS OF WHAT WOULD PRODUCE Pathways to Housing come accompanied by a single-word Greek chorus: preposterous! To understand why, we have to return to the "social imaginary" of an earlier time and place: New York City, late 1980s. At that time, the tone of the debate over outreach to the "homeless mentally ill" (officially launched by an American Psychiatric Association Task Force publication by that title in 1984) was perhaps best captured by local headlines like the one chronicling the antics of "the Wild Man of 96th Street." What passed for clinical subtlety was exemplified in an article exploring housing as "leverage" to be wielded in the service of behavior change. Its name says it all, but just to be clear: what made "Choices" (the original research demonstration of a drop-in center which led to Pathways to Housing; see Tsemberis et al. 2003) distinctive was the way it redefined the terms of debate over the street-dwelling homeless. It did this not by extending and camouflaging the police powers of psychiatry but by taking the absurd risk of meeting people (naked, unaccommodated, and all but unaccounted for) where they were, and exploring what might be done, on their own terms, to ease their lot.

A still-evolving experiment in social engineering—turning market self-interest to social good, albeit with an increasingly scarce stock of affordable housing—Pathways can claim (at least partial) credit for three developments.

1. A wholesale *rethinking* of the project of psychiatric outreach to the street-dwelling homeless, breaking out of what had been two reciprocally defining antinomies. Cruelly caricatured, these were, on the one side, love's labor of endless engagement (exemplified in the preternatural patience of Goddard Riverside's Project Reachout),

and on the other side, the swift and peremptory practice of "body-snatching" (New York City's Project HELP's attempt to "persuade" seriously impaired people to come in from the cold . . . and sample Bellevue's hospitality). Dignity fought it out with efficiency, each wielding a miserly stock of goods to help tip the outcome. Pathways essentially turned outreach on its head: instead of a demand-side approach (persuasion or coercion), it focused on the supply side of a valued good: a place of one's own.What it showed was how, honored in this least salubrious of settings, even a *lumpen* preference could become vested stake; leveraged preference morphed into prized possession. Offered secure and affordable housing, even people notorious for their unusual wants and self-injurious pride *will somehow find a way* (with a little help from their Pathways friends) to hold onto what they've claimed. It wasn't just that carrot trumped stick; self-respect got the better of unanswered grievance.

2. At the same time, the *practice* of (first Choices, and later) Pathways workers has prompted several attempts to rework standard analyses of choice and coercion. Too complicated to gloss here, this reworking is best exemplified in the work of Anne Lovell (Lovell 1992, 1996; Lovell & Cohn 1998; also Hopper 2006; Luhrmann 2008).

3. But perhaps most important and least appreciated is what Pathways has taught us about effective dissemination in an unreceptive, if not actively hostile, social imaginary. One thing is clear: evidence ain't enough. The early publications from Choices (Shern et al. 2000) were unmistakably positive; they also emphasized that lack of affordable housing would be the rate-limiting step. But *no one*, least of all the architects and bankers of mental health policy, was convinced by mere comparative effectiveness to reconsider the protocols of street outreach. And there the story would have ended, another chapter in the sorry annals of demonstration projects whose initial promise was met with official neglect, had it not been for Sam Tsemberis' foolhardy (if redemptive) move to reinvent himself as a housing provider and grab the bureaucratic bull by the horns.

Wresting piecemeal funding on a trial basis, he was eventually able to parlay that into durable contracts. Once the comparative data on *costs* started rolling in (Gulcur et al. 2003), effectiveness was wed to economy and a wholly different interest was piqued (which explains the unlikely attention of the Bush White House). And the rest, as they say, will one day be history.

Kim Hopper, Ph.D.
Research Scientist, Nathan Kline Institute for Psychiatric Research
Professor, Mailman School of Public Health, Columbia University

I FIRST ENCOUNTERED Housing First in a meaningful way when I phoned Sam Tsemberis in the spring of 2008 to describe the $110 million research demonstration project that had just been funded by Health Canada. The idea was to implement and evaluate a program for those who are homeless and mentally ill, but we had an open book regarding the intervention to be studied and the design that would be used. My quick scan of the recent research literature confirmed that some combination of assertive community treatment (act) and housing had the strongest evidence base (Nelson et al., 2007); the randomized controlled trial that had been completed by Pathways was the most frequently cited study. I also knew that Housing First had been endorsed by our federal homeless initiative and was already in play in at least two Canadian cities, Calgary and Toronto. But I was unsure what all the fuss was about: what made this program model different from other supportive housing models?

Hence the phone call with Sam. That conversation and the quick e-mail messages that followed convinced me that there was something special about this approach—one that combined a radical recovery orientation with a sensible, evidence-informed housing-plus-service model. So we chose it as the intervention to be implemented in a five-city trial across Canada, and as we have explained, defended, and put it into practice, I can say I am pleased with our decision. We now have nine act and intensive case management (icm) service teams as well as five unique service variations, all working with housing procurement teams to provide services to hundreds of formerly homeless, mentally ill participants. Our mixed methods study will add to our knowledge base about the implementation and impact of Housing First in various contexts.

So what is special about Housing First? It clearly meets the definition of a complex intervention. It includes elements of supportive housing, assertive community treatment, harm reduction, and recovery-oriented care. These program elements are combined in a sequence that puts housing before anything else and builds upon a value base that honors choice from start to finish. It arose from a fervent desire to do a better job of helping individuals with severe mental illness to get off the streets and out of a shelter system that had become another institutional catch-all for a seemingly intractable social problem. In addition to the entrepreneurial spirit that refused to let a good thing die, its origins and progress reflect a unique combination of pragmatic and philosophical concerns. The core elements of the model's success are lots of on-the-ground experience with what works—formalized in research-generated evidence—plus a fierce dedication to humane care that places the client in the center of the action and decision making.

It is hard to separate the program from the leader who created and championed it. Sam and his excellent staff embody the substance and spirit of the approach. Because they have also systematically evaluated and described it, it now has a life of its own. This manual helps define more clearly how the program theory can be operationalized. But Pathways is not, strictly speaking, a technology. It is a radically new way of doing business that cannot be put into place using a "by the book" mentality. Because of its complexity, it will need to be adapted to the particular population and context where is it being used. So this manual will work best as a guide, not a Bible, for those who wish to try this program model. Steering a careful course between standardization and adaptation will ensure that the essence of providing housing and support in ways that honor tenants' choices is maintained, while the local details may vary. We have found that training and technical assistance by experienced practitioners alert to local circumstances is a critical piece of the implementation process. We hope that our evaluation, and those of others who are also learning by doing, will eventually lead to many extensions and revisions of a program manual that only makes sense as part of a social movement.

Paula Goering, R.N., Ph.D.
Research Lead, Mental Health Commission
    of Canada At Home/Chez Soi project
Professor, University of Toronto

Appendix G

Additional Resources

Pathways to Housing, Inc.

Pathways National Office
55 West 125ᵗʰ Street, Floor 10
New York, NY 100027
212-289-0000
info@pathwaystohousing.org
www.pathwaystohousing.org

For locations in other cities, visit the above Web site.

Other Organizations and Agencies

These organizations' Web sites host useful information on issues concerning home-lessness, mental health, and addiction.

- National Alliance to End Homelessness: www.endhomelessness.org

- U.S. Department of Health and Human Services Substance Abuse and Mental Health Services Administration: www.samhsa.gov

- U.S. Department of Housing and Urban Development: www.hud.gov

- U.S. Interagency Council on Homelessness: www.ich.gov

Other Hazelden Resources

Behavioral Health Evolution Web site: *www.bhevolution.org.* This site offers innovative resources and expert advice on treating mental health, addiction, and co-occurring disorders; it also includes updates on Pathways Housing First.

Co-occurring Disorders Program: Integrated Services for Substance Use and Mental Health Problems, developed by faculty from the Dartmouth Medical School (Center City, MN: Hazelden, 2008)

Double Trouble in Recovery by Howard Vogel (Center City, MN: Hazelden, 2010)

Publications under the Dartmouth PRC—Hazelden Imprint

IDDT—Integrated Dual Disorders Treatment: Best Practices, Skills, and Resources for Successful Client Care by Lindy Fox, Kim Mueser, and other Dartmouth Psychiatric Research Center staff (Center City, MN: Hazelden, 2008)

Illness Management Recovery (IMR) by Kim Mueser and Susan Gingrich (Center City, MN: Hazelden, Fall 2011)

The Integrated Dual Disorders Treatment Recovery Life Skills Program by Lindy Fox with staff from the Dartmouth Psychiatric Research Center (Center City, MN: Hazelden, Spring 2011)

Supported Employment: Applying the Individual Placement and Support (IPS) Model to Help Clients Compete in the Workforce (updated and expanded edition), by Sarah J. Swanson and Deborah R. Becker (Center City, MN: Hazelden, March 2011)

Notes

1. Adapted from a United Nations publication (1998), "Principles and Recommendations for Population Housing Censuses," paragraph 1.328.

2. Shah, Ajit (2009). "The Relationship Between Socio-economic Status and Mental Health Funding, Service Provision, and National Policy: A Cross-national Study," *International Psychiatry* 6:2, April 2009, www.rcpsych.ac.uk/pdf/IPv6n2 .pdf#page=20.

3. Shinn, M. (2007). "International Homelessness: Policy, Socio-cultural, and Individual Perspectives," *Journal of Social Issues* 63, 659–679.

4. *2007 Annual Homeless Assessment Report,* U.S. Department of Housing and Urban Development, Office of Community Planning and Development, July 2008.

5. *2007 National Law Center on Homelessness and Poverty Annual Report,* 5.

6. Link, Bruce, et al. (1994). "Lifetime and Five-Year Prevalence of Homelessness in the United States" in *American Journal of Public Health,* December 1994.

7. *2007 Annual Homeless Assessment Report.*

8. Canadian Institute for Health Information (2007). *Improving the Health of Canadians: Mental Health and Homelessness Summary Report,* August 30, 2007, http://secure.cihi.ca /cihiweb/en/downloads/mental_health_sum mary_aug22_2007_e.pdf.

9. Ghosh, A. (2003). "Down and Out in Europe," *Time Magazine,* Feb. 10, 2003, www.time.com/time/europe/magazine /2003/0210/homeless/story.html.

10. Baker, Sherryl, et al. (2000). "Tenure in Supportive Housing for Homeless Persons with Severe Mental Illness," *Psychiatric Services* 51, 479–486.

11. O'Hara, Ann (2007). "Housing for People with Mental Illness: Update of a Report to the President's New Freedom Commission," *Psychiatric Services* 58, 907–913.

12. Appelbaum, Paul, et al. (2001). "Mandated Community Treatment: Beyond Outpatient Commitment," *Psychiatric Services* 52, 1198–1205.

13. Allen, Michael (2003). "Waking Rip Van Winkle: Why Developments in the Last

20 Years Should Teach the Mental Health System Not to Use Housing as a Tool of Coercion." *Behavorial Sciences and the Law* 21, 503–521.

14. Gordon, Lawrence, et al. (1995). "Housing Choice and Community Success for Individuals with Serious and Persistent Mental Illness," *Community Mental Health Journal* 31, 139–152.

15. New Freedom Commission on Mental Health (2003). *Achieving the Promise: Transforming Mental Health Care in America—Final Report.* Rockville, MD: DHHS Pub. No. SMA-03-3832.

16. More information on the ACT Fidelity Scale can be found at the SAMHSA Web site: http://download.ncadi.samhsa.gov/ken/pdf /toolkits/community/16.ACT_Fidelity_Scale .pdf.

17. National Association of State Mental Health Program Directors (2006) report, http://www.nasmhpd.org/general_files /publications/med_directors_pubs /technical%20report%20on%20morbidity %20and%20mortaility%20-%20final %2011-06.pdf.

18. Illness Management and Recovery is another of SAMHSA's evidence-based practices. See www.mentalhealth.samhsa.gov /cmhs/communitysupport/toolkits/illness.

19. For more information, see Becker, D. R., et al. (2001). "Fidelity of Supported Employment Programs and Employment Outcomes," *Psychiatric Services* 52, 834–836. See also the SAMHSA Supported Employment Toolkit at www.mentalhealth. samhsa.gov/cmhs/CommunitySupport /toolkits/employment/default.aspx.

20. For more information on IDDT, see the SAMHSA toolkit at http://mentalhealth .samhsa.gov/cmhs/CommunitySupport /toolkits/cooccurring/default.aspx. An expanded and updated edition of *IDDT, Integrated Dual Disorders Treatment: Best Practices, Skills, and Resources for Successful Client Care,* by Lindy Fox, Kim Mueser, and other Dartmouth Psychiatric Research Center staff, has been published under the Dartmouth PRC–Hazelden imprint (Center City, MN: Hazelden, 2010).

21. Stein, L. I., and Test, M. A. (1980). "An Alternative to Mental Health Treatment. I: Conceptual Model, Treatment Program, and Clinical Evaluation," *Archives of General Psychiatry* 37, 392–397.

22. Dr. Charles Rapp (1993), in Maxine Harris and Helen Bergman, *Case Management for Mentally Ill Patients: Theory and Practice* (Amsterdam: Harwood, 1993).

23. Updated and expanded editions of *IDDT* and *Supported Employment* have also been published by Hazelden under the Dartmouth PRC–Hazelden imprint, and a new edition of *IMR* will be available in June 2011.

24. Tatarsky, Andrew, and Marlatt, G. Alan (2010). "State of the Art in Harm Reduction Psychotherapy: An Emerging Treatment for Substance Misuse," *Journal of Clinical Psychology* 66:2 (Feb. 2010), 117–122.

25. DTR is registered on SAMHSA's National Registry of Evidence-Based Programs and Practices. Educational materials have been published by Hazelden to aid professionals in selecting and training peer leaders and maintaining groups in their facilities or communities.

References

Bendixen, A. (2008). *Chicago Housing for Health Cost Analyses.* Paper presented at the Third National Housing and HIV/AIDS Research Summit, Baltimore, Maryland.

Dunbeck, D. (July 2006). *Housing Chronically Homeless People: Housing First Programs in Philadelphia,* National Alliance to End Homelessness Annual Conference, Washington, DC.

Greenwood, R. M., Shaefer-McDaniel, N. J., Winkel, G., and Tsemberis, S. J. (2005) "Decreasing Psychiatric Symptoms by Increasing Choice in Services for Adults with Histories of Homelessness." *American Journal of Community Psychology* 36 (3/4), 223–238.

Gulcur, L., Stefancic, A., Shinn, M., Tsemberis, S., and Fischer, S. N. (2003). "Housing, Hospitalization, and Cost Outcomes for Homeless Individuals with Psychiatric Disabilities Participating in Continuum of Care and Housing First Programmes." *Journal of Community and Applied Social Psychology* 13, 171–186.

Hirsch, E., and Glasser, I. (2008). "Rhode Island's Housing First Program: Year 1 Evaluation Executive Summary." Available online at www.rihomeless.com/Press%20 Releases/Housing%20First%20Rhode%20 Island%20Report%20-%20Ex%20Summary. pdf.

Hopper, K. (2006). "Redistribution and Its Discontents: On the Possibility of Committed Work in Public Mental Health and Like Settings." *Human Organization* 65 (2), 218–226.

HUD/HHS/VA Collaborative Initiative to Help End Chronic Homelessness (2007). "National Performance Outcomes Assessment: Is System Integration Associated with Client Outcomes?" (Authors: Mares, Alvin; Greenberg, Greg; and Rosenheck, Robert.) June 15, 2007. Available at http://aspe.hhs.gov/hsp /homelessness/CICH07/integration/report .pdf; see also http://aspe.hhs.gov/_/topic /topic.cfm?topic=Homelessness.

Lovell, A.M. (1992). "Seizing the Moment: Power, Contingency, and Temporality in Street Life." In Rutz, H. (ed.), *The Politics of Time* (Washington DC: American Ethnological Society).

Lovell, A.M. (1996). "Coercion and Social Control: A Framework for Research on Aggressive Strategies in Community Mental Health." In Dennis, D.L. and Monahan, J., eds., *Coercion and Aggressive Community Treatment* (New York: Plenum).

Lovell, A.M., and Cohn, S. (1998). "The Elaboration of 'Choice' in a Program for Homeless Persons Labeled Psychiatrically Disabled." *Human Organization* 57 (1), 8–20.

Luhrmann, T.M. (2008). "'The Street Will Drive You Crazy': Why Homeless Psychotic Women in the Institutional Circuit in the United States Often Say No to Offers of Help." *American Journal of Psychiatry* 15 (1), 15–20.

Meschede, T. (2004). "Bridges and Barriers to Housing for Chronically Homeless Street Dwellers: The Effects of Medical and Substance Abuse Services on Housing Attainment." Retrieved February 14, 2007, from www.mccormack.umb.edu/centers/csp /publications/bridgesandbarriers.pdf.

National AIDS Housing Coalition (2008). "HIV/AIDS Housing: A Sound Investment of Public Resources."

Nelson, G., Aubry, T. and Lafrance, A. (2007). "A Review of the Literature on the Effectiveness of Housing and Support, Assertive Community Treatment, and Intensive Case Management Interventions for Persons with Mental Illness Who Have Been Homeless." *American Journal of Orthopsychiatry* 77 (3), 350–357.

Padgett, D. K. (2007). "There Is No Place Like (a) Home: Ontological Security Among Persons with Serious Mental Illness in the United States." *Social Science and Medicine* 64(9), 1925–1936.

Perlman, J., and Parvensky, J. (December 11, 2006). Denver Housing First Collaborative. "Cost Benefit Analysis and Program Outcomes Report." Denver, CO: Colorado Coalition for the Homeless. Retrieved Oct. 29, 2007, from www.shnny.org/documents /FinalDHFC CostStudy.pdf.

Sadowski, L. (2008). "Chicago Housing for Health Partnership: Background, Methods, and Preliminary Findings." Paper presented at the Third National Housing and HIV/AIDS Research Summit, Baltimore, MD.

Shern, D.L., Tsemberis, S., Anthony, W., Lovell, A.M., Richmond, L., Felton, C.J., Winarski, J., and Cohen, M. (2000). "Serving Street-Dwelling Individuals with Psychiatric Disabilities: Outcomes of a Psychiatric Rehabilitation Clinical Trial." *Psychiatric Services* 90 (12), 1873–1878.

Siegel, C. E., et al. (2006). "Tenant Outcomes in Supported Housing and Community Residences in New York City." *Psychiatric Services* 57:7, 982–991.

Srebnik, D. (October 2007). *Begin at Home: A Housing First Pilot Program.* Washington State Co-Occurring Disorders Conference, Yakima, WA.

Stefancic, A., and Tsemberis, S. (2007). "Housing First for Long-Term Shelter Dwellers with Psychiatric Disabilities in a Suburban County: A Four-Year Study of Housing Access and Retention." *Journal of Primary Prevention* 28(3/4), 265–279.

Tsemberis, S. (1999). "From Streets to Homes: An Innovative Approach to Supported Housing for Homeless Adults with Psychiatric Disabilities." *Journal of Community Psychology* 27 (2), 225–241.

Tsemberis, S., and Eisenberg, R. F. (2000). "Pathways to Housing: Supported Housing for Street-Dwelling Homeless Individuals with Psychiatric Disabilities." *Psychiatric Services* 51(4), 487–493.

Tsemberis, S., Gulcur, L., and Nakae, M. (2004). "Housing First, Client Choice, and Harm Reduction for Homeless Individuals with a Dual Diagnosis." *American Journal of Public Health* 94(4), 651–656.

Tsemberis, S., Moran, L.L., Shinn, M., Asmussen, S. M., and Shern, D. L. (2003). "Consumer Preference Programs for Homeless Individuals with Psychiatric Disabilities: A Drop-In Center and a Supported Housing Program." *American Journal of Community Psychology* 32, 305–317.

U.S. Department of Housing and Urban Development (July 2007). "The Applicability of Housing First Models to Homeless Persons with Serious Mental Illness: Final Report" (Authors: Abt Associates Inc.; Buron, Larry; Locke, Gretchen; Montgomery, Ann Elizabeth; Pearson, Carol L.; Walter R. McDonald & Associates, Inc.). Available at www.huduser.org/Publications/pdf/hsgfirst.pdf.

Yanos, P. T., Barrow, S. M., and Tsemberis, S. (2004). "Community Integration in the Early Phase of Housing among Homeless Persons Diagnosed with Severe Mental Illness: Successes and Challenges." *Community Mental Health Journal,* 40(2), 133–150.

Index

About the Author

Dr. Sam Tsemberis, founder of Pathways to Housing, Inc. and creator of the Pathways Housing First (PHF) model, grew up in Skouras, a small Greek village where families welcomed their mentally ill relatives unconditionally, shared their homes and meals with them, and valued them as contributing members of the community. Small wonder the idea of housing dual-disordered individuals in the wider community would, later on, come naturally to him.

After he earned his Ph.D. in clinical psychology, Dr. Tsemberis decided to act on these long-held values and his unwavering belief that housing is a basic right for *all* people. In 1992 he received a $500,000 grant from the New York State Office of Mental Health, which allowed him to make fifty apartments in Hell's Kitchen and Harlem available to homeless individuals with psychiatric disabilities and substance use disorders. From then until now, Dr. Tsemberis has remained faithful to the model he created and put into practice at Pathways to Housing—a model wherein treatment is offered to tenants, but is not a prerequisite for admission to the PHF program.

In 2007, the PHF program was entered into the National Registry of Evidence-based Programs maintained by the U.S. Department of Health and Human Services' Substance Abuse and Mental Health Services Administration (SAMHSA). Today, PHF programs have been replicated in more than one hundred cities across the United States, and a growing number of programs are in place in Canada and in Europe. Dr. Tsemberis and Pathways have been honored by the National Alliance to End Homelessness, the Center for Mental Health Services, the New York State Association for Psychiatric Rehabilitation, and others. In October 2005, the American Psychiatric Association Institute on Psychiatric Services recognized

Pathways to Housing with its prestigious Gold Award in the area of community mental health.

Dr. Tsemberis is on the faculty of the department of psychiatry of the Columbia University Medical Center. He has served as principal investigator for federally funded studies of homelessness, mental illness, and substance abuse, and has published numerous articles and book chapters on these topics. Dr. Tsemberis and Pathways to Housing have been profiled by NPR's *All Things Considered* and the *Newshour with Jim Lehrer,* and featured in the *New York Times,* the *Christian Science Monitor,* and most recently the *Chronicle of Philanthropy.* As founder and chief executive officer of Pathways to Housing, Inc., he serves as an international spokesperson on homelessness and the Housing First model of service. He is also the lead trainer and consultant for the Pathways Housing First Training Institute, which provides training and technical assistance to agencies throughout the world that seek to implement the PHF approach.